The Building of
Southampton Docks

Dave Marden

The Building of
Southampton Docks

Dave Marden

First published in Great Britain in 2012 by The Derby Books Publishing Company Limited, 3 The Parker Centre, Derby, DE21 4SZ.

ISBN 978-1-78091-062-8

Printed and bound by Copytech (UK) Limited, Peterborough.

Contents

Acknowledgements

In compiling this book I have sought to explain how and when the docks came about, their historical development, and the way they were constructed. This has been something of a balancing act between explaining the methods used, while at the same time, not overburdening the reader with excessive technical detail. It is hoped that the descriptions and illustrations will be enough to generate the reader's interest and unravel a few 'mysteries' as to how it all became what it is. From the early problems and setbacks to the later engineering triumphs, the story has unfolded over many lifetimes and will, no doubt, be there to see for many more in the future.

Much of the material contained in this volume has been made available through the good offices of Associated British Ports and, unless otherwise credited, all maps and photographs are their copyright. I'm also grateful for access to collections and individual items held by Jeff Pain, Jim Brown and Tony Chilcott, as well as friends and former work colleagues, and I apologise for any unintentional infringement of anyone else's copyright, which is purely accidental.

Obviously, the early days of the docks development were before the advent of commercial photography, and even where photographic records do exist it will be appreciated that much of this material has been in store for around 80 years or more and, in some cases, lacks the quality of modern day images. Some of the photographs may be familiar but most will not have been published before and I have sought to include those I feel are most informative and best illustrate how things were done.

The experience and knowledge imparted by my good friend Mr Bert Moody has been invaluable. Along with items from his extensive collection he provided much information and enlightenment from his many years of association with the docks and the vessels that graced its quays over several generations.

Dave Marden, 2012

Introduction

To most Southampton citizens, and indeed many visitors, the view of the Docks on its doorstep is a familiar sight witnessed daily without much of a second thought – as if it has always been there. I suppose to most of us it has and, apart from the addition of the container port from the late 1960s, nobody other than octogenarians will have witnessed any major changes in their lifetimes. Certainly, things have altered beyond recognition inside the docks themselves but to the casual observer and the mildly interested outsider, it has sat there, established and constant throughout their lifetimes. Nowadays it is impossible to imagine Southampton without its docks but there was a time, just over a century and a half ago, when it was not there at all.

Countless books have been written about the docks and many have referred to various stages of its development, but few have told the fuller story of its evolution from a couple of small basins clawed from the mud until it became the enormous industrial estate it is today. With the aid of early maps and photographs it is possible to illustrate the various stages of its growth and progress under various owners over the passage of time, and also, how it was built. In the earliest days muscle power was supplied by men and horses which, to some extent, were replaced by steam traction in the form of locomotives and heavy machinery. The development of the railways and advent of the steam navvy provided great advances to the heavy construction industry.

From the earliest days of its commencement under the ownership of the Southampton Dock Company, the docks has seen constant and continuous growth, both in size and in the facilities provided. The original two small basins soon proved inadequate, as did many of the extensions, due to the rapidly growing size of vessels and the evolution from modest sailing ships to giant ocean going liners.

The growth of shipping became so rapid that such a small concern could no longer sustain the finances necessary to keep it at the forefront of maritime requisites and only its transfer, in 1892, into the ownership of the powerful London & South Western Railway Company saved it from becoming an obsolete backwater. Under railway ownership, bigger, wider and deeper became the watchwords as each new phase of dock development unfolded. Within 20 years of the LSWR accession Southampton grew from a small docks to a huge port, but that is only half the story.

The regrouping of the railway companies in 1923 saw possession pass to the Southern Railway under whose tenure the docks doubled in size with the vast extension of the New Docks across the West Bay. The post-war nationalisation in 1948 saw further changes under state ownership with the eventual decline of passenger numbers due to air travel and the advent of containerisation. The initial quays of the container port opened in 1968, and then its final expansion to Redbridge in 1996 under private owners Associated British Ports, brings the story up date.

Southampton Docks from the air in 2005 with the Eastern Docks in the foreground, Western Docks in the centre, and the Container Port beyond. The triangle of trees in the centre right is Queens Park.

Part One
– The Early Docks

1. The Inner and Outer Docks

Southampton is blessed with double tides, a phenomenon created by the nearby Isle of Wight which creates two surges of the sea up Southampton Water, therefore creating advantageous conditions for shipping but, from medieval times, facilities at the town had been limited to small landings at the West Quay and Chapel Wharf, while the Town Quay was a mere stub of a jetty and a few passenger packet steamers plied to and from the Victoria Pier from 1833. Much of the trade in the early 1800s had been through wharves along the River Itchen but these were restricted by tidal mud and became inadequate for the growing size of vessels.

On 26th February 1831 a meeting was held to form the Southampton, London and Branch Railway and Dock Company with the object of providing a dock at Southampton and having direct links to London by rail. However, initial interest was muted, and, while the railway project eventually succeeded under the London and Southampton Railway, construction of the dock was left to others.

With the impending arrival of the railway, and its ensuing direct links with major towns and cities across the country, the prospect of a commercial dock at Southampton became an attractive proposition. The Harbour Commissioners responsible for the existing facilities could not raise the necessary capital but interest was such that an Act of Parliament, with an authorised capital of £350,000, was passed in May 1836 upon the formation of the Southampton Dock Company. Some 50 businessmen from London, Liverpool, Manchester and Southampton met at the George and Vulture Tavern in Lombard Street, London on 16th August that year where the chairman of the company announced that 216 acres had been acquired at a cost of £5,000. The area chosen was off the Town Beach, where the rivers of Test and Itchen met in a muddy confluence, the landward area being mainly marshland bounded by a promenade that today is Canute Road.

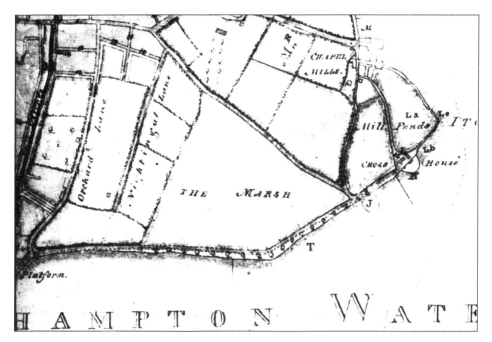

The area chosen for the docks construction was the Town Beach, originally a bleak shoreline between mud and marshland. The Platform Battery is at the bottom left with Crosshouse on the right.

The laying of the foundation stone was carried out with great ceremony on 12th October 1838, performed by a host of local dignitaries headed by the Mayor and Corporation and the local Masonic orders in full regalia. The ensemble paraded through the lower town before reaching the appointed place where some 20,000 souls (almost the entire local population) were gathered to witness the event. The stone was laid with due ritual by the Deputy Provincial Grand Master of Hampshire, Admiral Sir Lucius Curtis, with an inscribed silver trowel presented to him by the Dock Company. A similar item was also presented to Joseph Liggins, Chairman of the Company.

The stone contained a small cavity, sealed with a marble plate, into which was interred a number of gold, silver and copper coins. There followed a royal salute from the nearby gunnery at the Platform, after which the VIPs and notables headed back to the town for suitable celebrations.

The scene as the foundation stone was laid at what is now the north-west boundary of the Eastern Docks. The townsfolk cheer as smoke billows from guns at the Platform Battery at the centre of the picture. The distant God's House and the Town Quay are seen beyond.

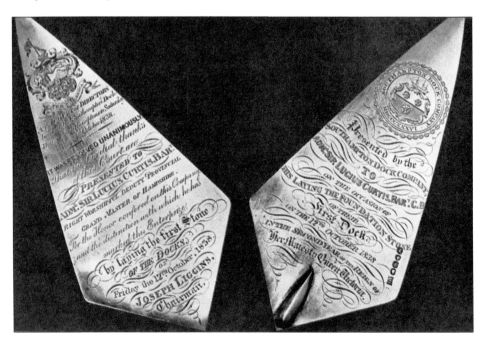

The obverse and reverse faces of the ceremonial trowel used by Admiral Sir Lucius Curtis during the laying of the docks foundation stone. The silver hallmarks can be seen along the right-hand side. (Dave Marden Collection)

Work commenced in the autumn of 1838 under the direction of engineer Francis Giles who had previously been associated with the building of the London and Southampton Railway. Giles had encountered problems in both construction and finance, and, being relieved of his situation, was free to be engaged at the docks where he was assisted by his son Alfred who later succeeded him as Dock Engineer upon his father's death on 4th March 1847.

The early days were fraught with problems. The initial plan was to build a quay wall from the shore and surround the construction area with cofferdams, an enclosure of piling whereby the inside water is pumped out to allow dry working inside, but after an expenditure of some £7,000, work was halted for several months through lack of finance. By the time it resumed in 1840, the plans had altered to accommodate the new Royal Mail Company steamers then being built, their size being somewhat larger than those existing at the time of the original dock designs. The overall scheme was for two docks, one tidal and another enclosed.

During this period Francis Giles had drawn up plans for a similar arrangement of a tidal and an enclosed dock at another location. This was further up the River Itchen at Northam where a drawing dated November 1839 shows the tidal dock entrance in the area of Millbank Wharf. That basin, and the enclosed dock that connected via a lock gate, would have taken up the land now occupied by Clarence Street, George Street, Kent Street, and Cable Street, reaching almost across to Northam Road. The docks would have been connected to the main railway line with a siding that ran to a point to the north of the Belvidere Shipyard.

It should be emphasised that in those days the localities of both Northam and Chapel were still rural, open fields with hardly a building in sight and it is difficult to imagine that orchards once lined Northam Road. Obviously, Giles' 'Plan B', if that's what it was, never materialised and work resumed at the original site.

Whereas it had been originally planned to build the first dock in stages, beginning with just the quay walls to accommodate the Royal Mail ships, it was decided to enclose the whole area with a mixture of earth banks and cofferdams to enable all berths to be created uniformly. In places, the original mud was up to 20 feet thick and this caused problems with the earth banks sinking between six and eight feet overnight. A severe storm occurred in November 1840 creating exceptional tides which breached the banks and flooded sections of the interior, thus preventing further excavation of the site in order to form more earthworks. The cofferdams were extended until the whole was watertight, the enclosure being completed in March 1841.

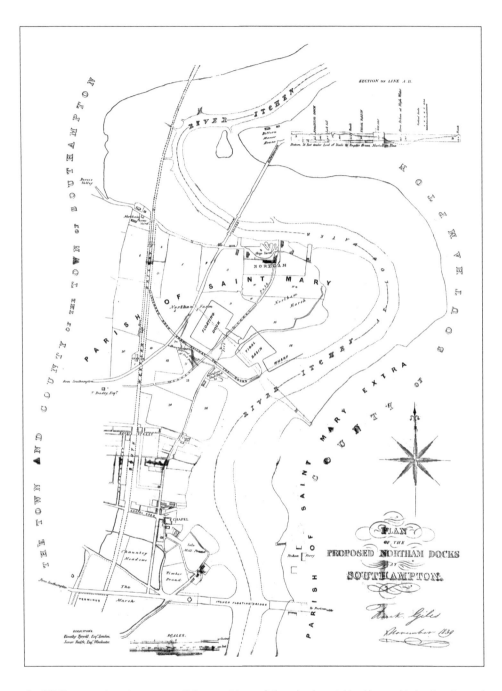

An 1839 map showing a possible re-siting of the docks at Northam. Note the line of the old town canal to its exit at the river adjacent to the Northam Shipyard (latterly Day & Summers). (Bert Moody Collection)

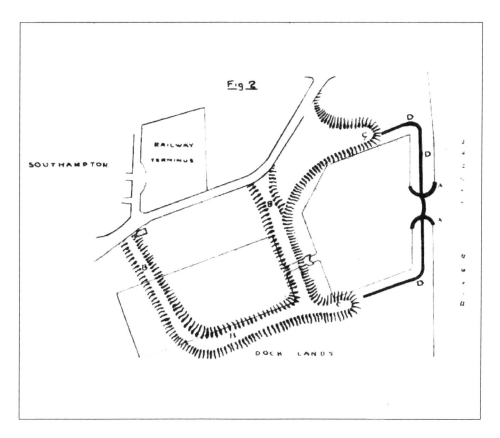

One of the original sketches for the Inner and Outer Docks showing the earthworks and cofferdams.

Excavation of the tidal dock then commenced, and some 1,150,000 cubic yards were removed in total. With work continuing day and night through the summer the horse roads and winding engines brought out as much as 3,500 cubic yards per day at a contracted price of 1s 2d per yard.

Trenches for the quay wall foundations were dug through a mixture of sandy clay, sand and quicksand, the infill being strengthened as appropriate. The masonry above them rose apace but before reaching its full height problems occurred with sections moving forward by up to three feet on a cushion of mud and clay. At this stage the dock was dry and pressure from the infill behind the walls was pushing them out. These sections were taken down and additional piling was applied to strengthen them before rebuilding could commence but the same problems manifested in other sections and the decision was taken to flood the dock in order to counterbalance the pressure from behind. Far from solving the issue, this made matters worse as the material behind the walls became saturated and the pressures increased, especially as the tide receded.

Several unsuccessful types of land ties, at costs totalling £10,000, were tried in an attempt to anchor the walls in place but all were doomed to failure. The problem was solved in the most part by removing spoil from behind the walls, thus creating voids and driving piles behind them, then building wooden platforms over their tops. This finally alleviated the outward pressure and rendered the quays above them operational. Despite everything, two P&O vessels, the *Tagus* and *Liverpool* berthed on 29th August 1842 and the 16 acre Tidal (Outer) Dock was formally opened on 1st July 1843.

The dock was initially used by the Royal Mail Steam Packet Company, which had trade routes to the West Indies, and the Peninsular & Oriental Steamship Company (P&O) who shipped passengers and cargoes to India.

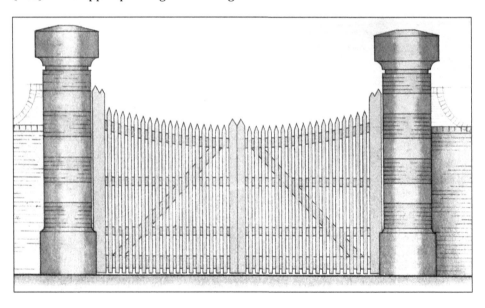

The original design drawing of the wooden gates for the Inner and Outer Docks. None of them survive but four of the original pillars remain in place along Canute Road. (Dave Marden Collection)

Opposite page top: A photograph showing rebuilding of the quay wall at No.3 berth in the Outer Dock in the late 1800s. Stone blocks are being hoisted by a steam crane mounted on a barge. To the right of the cargo shed is one of the dock residences. At this time it was occupied by the Superintendent of the Docks Police. (Dave Marden Collection)

A wonderful view of the docks inside the Canute Gate taken from the roof of a customs building that stood on the corner of Canute Road and Royal Crescent. It was before 1890 as there is no Empress Dock in the distance. The pathway runs from the gate to the steps at berth 1. In the foreground are the roofs of the police lodge and one time fire station. Berth 9 shed is the one on the left and the buildings at the centre and right of the photograph are warehouses and cargo sheds between the Inner and Outer Docks. The tall structure on the extreme right is E warehouse with the Inner Dock behind it. The railway shows some interesting vehicles, including a four-wheel van, while one of the Southampton Dock Company locomotives *Vulcan* stands beyond it. (Bitterne Local History Society Collection)

Looking south-east across vessels at the Outer Dock in 1910. In the foreground is the lock gate to the Inner Dock with its footbridge. The chimney on the right is that of the engine house for pumping the drydocks. (Dave Marden Collection)

As shipping increased there was an urgent need for repair facilities and the first of the company's graving, or drydocks, was built on the south side of the Outer Dock. This was constructed in stone and completed in 1846 at a cost of £49,800. Its floor length of 282 feet was increased to 343 feet in 1852 for an additional £1,800. Graving dock No.2 had a floor length of 252 feet and was built of brick and concrete at a much reduced cost of £19,290 in 1847. With further advances in ship's sizes the two drydocks were inadequate for many of the newer vessels and the decision was taken in 1853 to build a much bigger one, capable of taking the largest ships of the age. Built of brick, Drydock No.3 had a floor length of 424 feet and cost £53,000 when completed in December 1854.

An early photograph of the gates at No.1 Graving Dock. Looking north to the Outer Dock. Note the hydraulic quayside cranes.

The paddle steamer *Duchess of Albany* in No.2 Drydock. (Bert Moody Collection)

Another view looking north from the drydocks in 1904 shows vessels in the Outer Dock. A vessel is in No.3 Drydock on the right. (Dave Marden Collection)

The vessel *Rosyth* being overhauled at No.1 Drydock in 1930. The pumping station on the left served all three of the original drydocks. (Bert Moody Collection)

The Southern Railway Vessel *Ringwood* photographed in the Outer Dock on 6th July 1935, appears to be sitting across the entrance to the Inner Dock as the Baggage Warehouse B at berth 1 is behind its stern, while its bow is at berth 2. The tall building at the back is O Warehouse and on the far right is the former Continental Booking Office at berth 9. (Dave Marden Collection)

The next stage of dock development was to be the Inner, or Closed Dock, which would be linked to the Outer Dock via a lock gate. Construction had begun in 1840 with the initial excavations but limited finances again hindered progress and a decision was made to limit development to just two of the four planned quay walls, at the north and east of the dock, the others remaining as unmade gravel slopes until further funds were available. The quays along the north side measured 804 feet while the eastern quay measured 550 feet, including the dock entrance. Copious amounts of gravel removed from the excavations were used to construct concrete for the quay walls which were then faced with Purbeck stone. The 10 acre dock opened, in part, in late 1851 at a cost of £18,000 and this cost-efficient construction method was employed in later repairs in the Outer Dock. At that time, the south side of the dock was used for the lay-up of vessels, while jetties were built on the western side to accommodate the discharge of coal brigs.

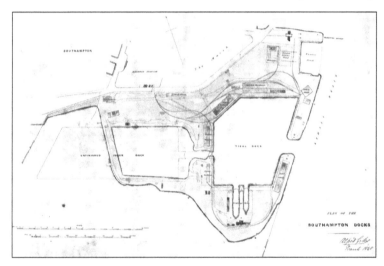

A drawing dated 1848 shows the Outer Dock complete with the first two graving docks along the south wall but the Inner Dock is still at the planning stage.

The entrance lock contained only one set of gates as the double tides allowed sufficient water for open access to the dock for two periods, each of three hours, per day. When the tide began to fall the men operating the gates had difficulty closing them against the flow of water so a 20 inch diameter sluice was built on the unmade south side of the dock to let out water and alleviate the pressure.

As work progressed on the Inner Dock it was soon realised that the entrance lock was far too restrictive to many classes of vessels using the port. The entrance was therefore widened and deepened to accommodate them. The original width had been 46 feet, more than ample for vessels in use at the planning stage some 20 years previous but by the time it had been brought into use the shipping world had moved on. Earlier regulations had also forbidden steamships to enter the lock gates due to the risk of fire but these had now been relaxed. The entrance was widened by 10 feet and the depth by four feet.

This handy piece of mechanism for opening the Inner Dock gate was built and installed by the local shipbuilders Summers & Day in 1855 and is seen here still in operation almost a century later.

The whole dock was soon considered too shallow to accommodate the current draft of many vessels and work commenced on 19th February 1858 to deepen the dock by a further five feet and to construct the south and west quays. These additional works saw the removal of 200,000 cubic yards of spoil and the pouring of 35,000 cubic yards of concrete and, together with the masonry facings and granite copes, the total cost of alterations ran to £60,000 by the time of completion. The sum also included the cost of suppers to the permanent men and a gratuity of 2s 0d each to the 80 labourers. On 20th May 1859 the dock was again open for business with the arrival of the P&O vessel *Pera*.

Looking west into the Inner Dock from the entrance in 1880. (Hume Family Collection /University of Queensland)

A further calamity had ensued when a combination of factors saw another wall (latterly that numbered as No.6 berth) in the Outer Dock collapse in January 1854, taking with it the shears (a hydraulic lifting device), resulting in a 120 foot section having to be rebuilt, which, together with the replacement of the shears, took 12 months at a cost of £11,500.

The Outer Dock quays were lined with wooden cargo sheds while stone warehouses were constructed around the Inner Dock. These were used for the storage of tobacco, grain, wines and spirits.

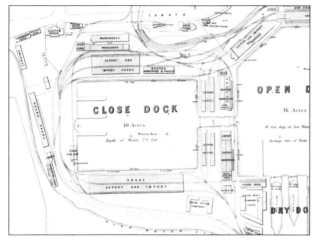

The Inner, or Close Dock in 1876 shows various sheds and warehouses from the early days with the lock entrance from the Open, or Outer Dock. Several of the buildings along Canute Road remain to this day.

Looking south across the Inner Dock showing only mud flats beyond where the Empress Dock was later built in 1890. (Dave Marden Collection)

A similar view around the turn of the century shows the later large warehouses in place to the north of the Inner Dock. The Empress Dock is visible in the centre distance, while the White Star Dock is yet to rise from the mud flats at the top right. (Jeff Pain Collection)

Vessels at the Inner Dock around 1910 with the Royal Mail Steam Packet Company's *Nile* and *Danube* laid up. Also to be seen is a three-masted schooner, a large steam yacht and, partly hidden behind the steamers, a three-masted barque. (Bert Moody collection)

An aerial view taken about 1920 shows vessels in the Inner Dock. The one on the right is alongside the grain warehouse being unloaded by suction equipment. This was the only non-tidal basin on the whole dock estate and the entrance lock can be seen in the foreground with the Terminus (Docks) railway station at the top right. (Bert Moody collection)

One of the original features at the Inner Dock was the hydraulic coal hoist at berth No.13 pictured on 1st December 1954. The structure finally disappeared when the dock was filled in during the 1960s. The vessel behind at berth No 14 is the naval training ship HMS *Wessex*.

Phase one of the great dock adventure was now complete and the Company Engineer Alfred Giles summed up its progress in an address to the Institution of Civil Engineers on 18th May 1858:

'The expenditure on the docks, drydocks, custom house, sugar refinery, workshops, warehouses, sheds, rails, and all other appliances up to the present time, has been £705,000. The gross return is £53,000 a year; and although the original shareholders may not have had much cause for congratulation, the dividend not having hitherto exceeded 4 per cent, the country at large has benefited, by the conversion of a huge mud bank, into a useful national work.'

A fourth drydock was deemed necessary to meet the growing needs of ship repairs and, with the existing three abreast taking up the south side of the Outer Dock, the new one was constructed outside, along the River Itchen and parallel with the others. When completed in December 1879 it was 450 feet long with 56 feet wide at entrance.

The German coaster *Golfstrom* under repair at No.4 Drydock in June 1980. This was the last vessel to use the dock which closed the following month. (Dave Marden)

Pictured on 13th July 1949, the first generation of drydocks on the south side of the Outer Dock. No.1 is on the right, containing the tug *Ashford*. No.2 in the centre, has the *Topmast No.10*. No.3 is unoccupied to the left, while the entrance to No.4 is on the far left on the River Itchen.

The original two basins, the Inner and Outer Docks, were largely obsolete by the 1960s due to their compact quaysides and lack of water depth at low tide. British Railways had been the principal user of the Outer Dock in latter years but moved its Channel Island passenger services to Weymouth in 1961, the last vessel from Southampton leaving on 12th May.

The Inner Dock had closed in 1963 but the Outer Dock gained something of a reprieve with the advent of drive on/drive off vessels. The Norwegian firm Thoresen Car Ferries commenced service from May 1964 after the dock was revamped for their coming and the cargo shed at berth 7 was modified for vehicle handling. The Inner Dock was filled in and the newly created ground became the marshalling area for vehicles using ferries at berths 2 and 3. The width of the Outer Dock entrance was doubled from 151 feet to 302 feet and new facilities were provided. Drydocks 1, 2 and 3 were filled in as part of the scheme, while number 4 remained in operation until closed at the end of July 1980 and was later swallowed up by the Ocean Village redevelopment in 1985.

Whether by consequence or competition, the British Rail continental services to Le Havre and St Malo had ended by September 1964 but cargo services continued from Southampton until transfer to Portsmouth in 1972.

The first major change in the docks quays for 30 years occurred with the revamp of the Inner and Outer Docks for the car ferry trade. At the bottom of the picture the Inner Dock has been filled in to provide a back up area for the marshalling of vehicles. At the top left of the photograph is the newly refurbished berth No.6 for Thoresen while in the centre, the new jetty at No.2 berth will provide facilities for Southern Ferries. The vessel at berth No.3 is the Swedish Lloyd ferry *Patricia*.

The Princess Alexandra Dock, now fully equipped for cross channel ferry operations, shows vessels at berths 2 (south) and 7, with the new waiting hall at berth 6 in the foreground. At the top of the picture, the former Inner Dock is now just a memory, the area serving as a marshalling area for the ferries. Barges laden with timber occupy the former coal barge dock at bottom right. On the left, No.3 drydock is in the process of being filled in.

A new waiting hall was provided for Thoresen at No.6 berth while another, at berth No.3, was opened on 3rd July 1967 when the dock was renamed Princess Alexandra Dock. In April that year the Swedish Lloyd vessel *Patricia* made its first sailing to Bilbao and, two months later, Normandy Ferries began services on 29th June.

Southern Ferries (later P&O Ferries) began sailings to Le Havre with their vessel *Dragon* and the *Leopard* entered service on 1st May 1968. Three years on their services had been extended to Lisbon and Casablanca with a larger ship named *Eagle* which made its maiden voyage on 18th May 1971. Additional ferry facilities were provided via link spans at berth 30 from 1976 and at berth 25 from 1988.

The boom in ferry services was relatively short lived as the Spanish service ended in 1977 and Thoresen had transferred their vessels to Portsmouth by 1983 with P&O Ferries following them a year later. There was a brief resumption in 1991 when Stena

Sealink introduced the *Stena Normandy* on a regular service to Cherbourg. Running from a redeveloped terminal at berth 30 the service proved very popular until 1996 when traffic declined and eventually ceased after the opening of the Channel Tunnel.

The ferry waiting hall at berths 2/3 when new in 1967. The site was later redeveloped as the Harbour Lights Cinema after the area became Ocean Village in the mid 1980s.

With the Inner Dock a distant memory, the Princess Alexandra Dock had last been used by ferries in 1984 and was now totally unsuitable to modern vessels and their requirements. The area that once formed the original dock estate was leased for development as a marina and leisure complex named Ocean Village in 1985 with the 75 acre site eventually being sold to new owners a few years later.

Ocean Village as it was in 1985 with houses and apartments, to the right, replacing the former old dockside buildings. The marina and Canute's Pavillion are established on the north side of the dock while redevelopment work continues on the south side, where the outline of the former No.4 drydock is visible in the left foreground.

2. The Itchen Quays

With the Inner and Outer Docks having been completed, and with trade now increasing still further, thoughts soon turned to expansion and several grand schemes were drawn up for additional docks. Some of these included a series of enclosed docks interlinked to the originals by further locks and gates. Presumably, the experiences of the Inner Dock gave rise to doubts, as all further dock extensions were tidal.

Of many plans drawn up for the expansion of the docks, this one in 1853 had three interlinked basins but experiences with the established Inner (or Close) Dock decided that, in future, all new docks would be tidal with open access to the sea.

The first new major work was an extension of quays, southwards, down the River Itchen from the Outer Dock. This was begun in 1873 and 2,000 feet of additional quays had been completed by 1876, the contractors being John Aird and Company. Whether this was with great foresight may be debated but the new construction formed one side of the future Empress Dock that was begun in 1886 and completed in 1890.

The Itchen Quay, extension could initially accommodate vessels with a draft of 20 feet but this was increased to 30 feet in 1905. Canadian Pacific and Rotterdam Lloyd ships used these berths, latterly numbered 30-33, while those of Royal Mail and P&O also made use of the new facilities.

The Itchen Quays looking north along the sheds at berths 31-32 in 1934. (Bert Moody Collection)

A drawing dated 1886 showing the extended quays down the River Itchen with thoughts for the Empress Dock already in mind.

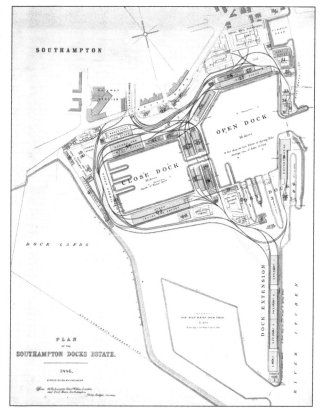

Below: The entrance to the Empress Dock with vessels at the Itchen Quays on the right of the photograph. (Jeff Pain Collection)

3. The Empress Dock

Initially, the Dock Company had insufficient funds to meet the cost of building a much needed new dock and made arrangements with the London & South Western Railway Company for a loan of £250,000. The railway was pleased to assist, as the increased trade from passengers and freight would no doubt lead to higher revenues that would, in turn, more than cover their investment. The contract for the Empress Dock was eventually awarded to S. Pearson and Son of London for a sum of £149,000.

In preparation, a sea bank enclosing the site was begun in August 1886 and completed in March 1887. Constructed from chalk and gravel it contained 185,000 cubic yards, while its length stretched for 3,000 feet and was a minimum 20 feet wide at the top. The total area enclosed by the bank was 42 acres and a total 1,042,000 cubic yards was excavated for the dock. Two large sumps were sunk to assist drainage during the works. One was 55 feet deep at the south west-corner, while the other, at the north east of the site had a depth of 60 feet. Both were equipped with powerful pumps to discharge water back into the sea.

Initial excavations were carried out by hand, filling wagons with mud which were tipped on the outside of the bank to help make it watertight. 100 foot wide trenches for the wall footings were started in November 1887 with the spoil removed at first by barrows, then later by horse roads. Crane and wagon roads were laid alongside the trenches after they had been shored by timbers, the contents being put into hand filled skips which were then hoisted and tipped into wagons for disposal. The wagons were worked up inclines by winding gear powered by portable engines at the north-east and north-west corners of the dock. At the top of the inclines the wagons were taken away by horses and locomotives for dumping as filling behind the north wall. Pearson's engaged at least four locomotives during the period of the works.

The materials packed behind walls paved the way for the return of an old spectre. Disaster struck once again as the north wall gave way in October 1888, moving vertically forward by as much as 21 feet over a length of 475 feet. Efforts to alleviate the problem saw large gangs of men removing the backing and dumping the material over the quay wall to form a barrier at its base. Elsewhere, concrete buttresses were sunk in front of the walls and the backing material was lightened, but all to no avail as the problems persisted. The north and east walls were eventually demolished by blasting with gunpowder and then rebuilt with extra piling at the toes. The cost of this remedial work ran between £30,000 and £40,000, which was shared equally between the Dock Company and the contractor.

The then monster dock had an area of 18 acres 3,854 feet of quays with its entrance being 175 feet wide and the dock would never have less than 26 feet of water whatever state of the tide. On completion of the quay walls the enclosing bank was removed and the dock flooded. The dock was then dredged to the required depth with the soil being taken away by steam hopper barges and dumped in deep water off Calshot. The quayside areas around the dock were ballasted with chalk and clay, with sheds erected in pairs around the north, west and south quays, and a single shed on the east quay. Each of these being 350 feet long, 120 feet wide and 28 feet high. The sheds were built on concrete piers and constructed of wood with slate roofs. The windows were aligned under the eaves, as skylights were considered difficult to keep watertight. These new berths later became numbered 20-27.

The dock was officially opened on 26th July 1890 by Her Majesty, Queen Victoria who arrived by sea from Cowes aboard the Royal Yacht *Alberta*, which broke a ceremonial ribbon stretched across the dock entrance. The event was witnessed by around 30,000 spectators who then saw the vessel steam slowly around the dock before mooring at what is now berth 20/1, where the monarch granted an audience to the Dock Company chairman and directors.

Upon receiving their address, Her Majesty responded:

'I receive with pleasure your loyal and dutiful address. It gives me great satisfaction to inaugurate this important addition to the Docks of Southampton and to see so striking an illustration of the energy of commercial enterprise in my kingdom. I trust the Port of Southampton will feel the benefit of the great work you have completed and will exhibit in the future increasing developments of trade and prosperity'.

To mark the occasion of naming the dock a large flag was unfurled from a high mast on the quayside. The standard displayed the arms of the Southampton Dock Company with the words 'Empress Dock 1890' – and, more interestingly, included the letters L. & S.W.R. The railway company did not, in fact, take over the docks until 1892 but its inclusion on the flag no doubt signified the close partnership of the two companies.

Once more Southampton Docks was at the forefront of progress with a facility that could take the largest vessels afloat at any state of the tide.

An excited crowd awaits the arrival of Queen Victoria as, in the distance, the Royal yacht *Alberta* steams in through the entrance to the Empress Dock on 26th July 1890. The two funnelled vessel in the background is the Royal Mail Steam Packet Company's *Magdalena* at berth 33 and, nearest the camera, is the Portsmouth steam paddler *Falcon*. The transit sheds on the south quays are still under construction in the centre of the photograph.

The flag, which marked the opening of the Empress Dock, measured 15 feet by 12 feet and is displayed here at the Eastern Docks Engineer's Yard in August 1950. Note the initials 'L. & S.W.R.' included two years before the railway company took ownership of the docks.

The 1930s saw the arrival of the Elders & Fyffes banana trade located at berth 25 where a system of elevators and conveyers carried the fruit from ships into the shed for onward transportation by specially equipped trains. In later years, British Railways ran cross channel cargo ships from berths 22 and 23.

Part of the Empress Dock was given over to the development of the Southampton Oceanography Centre (now the National Oceanography Centre) which was officially opened in April 1996. The centre is home to 520 scientists and over 700 students who research the maritime environment.

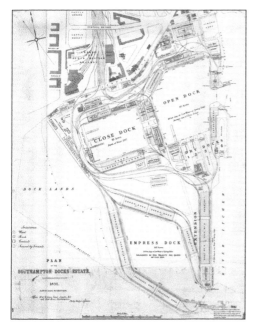

Left: The Eastern Docks begins to take on a more familiar shape with this 1891 drawing showing the Empress Dock almost completed after it had been officially opened the previous year.

Below: A view of the Empress Dock from the Prince of Wales drydock in the early 1900s shows vessels of three main shipping companies then using the port. On the left is the bow of the Royal Mail Steam Packet ship *Atrato*, built in 1888, moving across the centre is either the *New York* or *Philadelphia* of the American Line, while on the right is a Union Castle Mail ship believed to be either the *Kildonan Castle* or the *Kinfauns Castle*. The recess in the quay wall on the left was to accommodate the drydock caisson which swung open outwards. (Dave Marden collection)

The Empress Dock was used by Royal Mail Line's services to South America and later became the place of embarkation for troopships during conflicts and for many years afterwards in peacetime. It also handled the banana traffic of Elders & Fyffes ships for many years.

Vessels in the Empress Dock c.1912. (Dave Marden Collection)

The eve of war in 1939 with ships in the Empress Dock (centre). The *Queen Mary* is in the Ocean Dock beyond. while the Floating Drydock in the top distance would soon be moved to the Admiralty at Portsmouth Dockyard.

4. The Prince of Wales Drydock & Quays

Pressures on the dock company finances continued and eventually the undertaking was purchased by the LSWR on 1st November 1892, the price being £1,360,000. The new owners lost no time investing in their new acquisition with a contract for an additional drydock. Yet again this would be the biggest and best in the world.

In 1893 a contract was let to John Aird and Company for alterations to the southern quay wall of the Empress Dock to allow construction of the entrance to the graving dock, and also for building the dock itself. Further works by Aird included the provision of a coal dock, converted from a timber pond near the floating bridge (a steam operated chain ferry which ran across the River Itchen to the inceasingly populated neighbourhood of Woolston) and the redevelopment of adjacent cattle sheds and an abattoir as War Department stores for the Admiralty.

The new 745 feet long drydock was opened by the Prince of Wales (later Edward VII) on 3rd August 1895, by which time 1,642 feet of new quays had been completed southwards along the Itchen from the entrance of the Empress Dock. These were known as the Prince of Wales Quays and latterly numbered as berths 34-36, the coal dock and Admiralty stores being finished a year later.

Crowds swarm around the drydock entrance and across the caisson bridge at the opening of the Prince of Wales Drydock on 3rd August 1895. (Dave Marden collection)

The drydock itself followed the fate of its predecessors and closed in 1977 when, after becoming a landfill site, it was surfaced for export car storage. The Coal Barge Dock and the site of the old Admiralty Stores eventually became engulfed in the Ocean Village development of 1985.

Another early scene at the Prince of Wales Drydock has the *Carisbrooke Castle* high and dry around 1906. (Bert Moody Collection)

An unusual visitor to the Prince of Wales Drydock was the Southern Railway vessel *Hantonia* seen here on 10th June 1937. The railway vessels were normally serviced in the smaller drydocks. (Bert Moody Collection)

The Prince of Wales Quays (afterwards known as the Ocean Quay) had 28ft of water at low tide and became home to vessels of the Union Castle Line, whose services to South Africa brought imports of fruit, wool grain and animal skins. The old quaysides at berths 34-36 were rebuilt and widened by contractor Sir Robert McAlpine in 1939, and during these alterations, Union Castle switched their operations to berth 106 until the modified quays were reopened in February 1940.

A Union Castle ship at the Ocean Quay alongside the original wooden sheds at berth 34 in 1905. (Jeff Pain Collection)

The cargo sheds at berth 34 were reconstructed in brick, replacing the original wooden buildings around 1927. This photograph was taken about that time. (Bert Moody Collection)

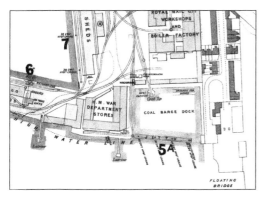

The newly created Coal Barge Dock and War Department Stores near the Floating Bridge. In 1896 referred to as berth 5A but afterwards renumbered as berth 28. The exposed latrines out over the River Itchen would not have been comfortable in cold weather.

Coal barges being loaded from a Cory Brothers collier at berth 28. Each of the four electrically operated cranes was capable of lifting five tons. However, such activity would be rare by the 1930s when the majority of liners became oil fired.

The contents of railway wagons were unloaded at the Coal Barge Dock tipping jetty, seen here in action c.1920. This would not have been the cleanest or healthiest occupation for those employed there.

The dilapidated wagon tipping jetty at the Coal Barge Dock was long out of use when this photograph was taken in 1975, and the barges shown here were used for transporting timber. The houses in the background were in Floating Bridge Road and the crane jibs behind them were engaged in the construction of the Itchen Bridge. (Dave Marden)

5. The Test Quays

The relentless changes under the railway company management continued with further extensions including the 425 feet South Quay (berth 37) where, on 12th October 1898, a commemorative stone was laid at the Dock Head to mark the 60th anniversary of the laying of the original foundation stone. The 2,227 feet Test Quays (berths 38-40) were all completed by 1902.

Additional berths at 41, 42, 48 and 49 were completed along with the White Star Dock (berths 43-47) in 1911, while berths 50-51 were in place after the completion of the Trafalgar Drydock.

The South Quay provided 30 feet of water at low tide and was used by vessels of Rotterdam Lloyd and the Netherland Royal Mail lines before Union Castle based their Continental steamers at that berth. The Test Quays had a minimum of 32 feet of water where the International Cold Storage Company's large cold store handled various commodities including fruit and eggs from Union Castle's South African service as well as produce from Argentina and New Zealand.

Throughout its history, Southampton Docks has been a major embarkation point for overseas conflicts. This photograph shows troops boarding a vessel at berth 40 bound for the Crimean War. (Jeff Pain Collection)

The steamship *Adriatic* at the Test Quays in the 1920s. The vessel was laid up in Liverpool in 1933 and scrapped in 1934-35. (Jeff Pain Collection)

The vessel *Braque* at berth 37 at the Dock Head in the 1960s when visitors were greeted with 'Southampton Docks' painted on the roof of the shed at berth 36. The old sheds at berths 38/39 on the left of the photograph were replaced by the Queen Elizabeth II Terminal in 1966. (Jeff Pain Collection)

A new passenger terminal was opened by Her Majesty the Queen on 15th July 1966 at berths 38/39. It was named in her honour as the Queen Elizabeth II Terminal and became the home base of the much loved Cunarder *QE2*.

The new QEII passenger terminal at berth 38/39 in 1966.

An early visitor to the new Queen Elizabeth II Terminal was the Union Castle Line's *Pendennis Castle*.

On 1st January 1963 the British Transport Commission was abolished and the British Transport Docks Board became an independent statutory authority on 1st August 1968, a year which saw a major change in the port's organisation when the Southampton Harbour Board was amalgamated with the Docks Board, the new body being responsible for the administration and conservancy of the whole port including Southampton Water.

In the independent days of the Harbour Board, the Port Signal and Radar Station had been located at Calshot Castle, but July 1972 saw the establishment of a new Port Communications Centre at the Dock Head berth 37.

Left: The new Port Communications Centre at Dock Head with the south end of the nearly new Queen Elizabeth II Terminal on the left.

Below: The official opening of the new Port Signal and Radar Station at berth 37 was performed by board member Mr R.F. Pugh on 7th July 1972. (Bert Moody Collection)

Times of change at the Test Quays where the Queen Elizabeth II Terminal stands on berth 38/39, with the new Port Communications Centre at the Dock Head. On the right are the original wooden sheds of the Ocean Quay at berth 35-36.

6. The Trafalgar Drydock

Following on from the building of the Test Quays, a chalk embankment was constructed around the perimeter of the docks estate enclosing the land, or sea bed, assigned for future expansion. This included the areas that are now Trafalgar Drydock and the Ocean Dock.

Contractor Aird's work had obviously impressed the dock owners as the firm was engaged for yet another mammoth project. With ever increasing pressures on the existing repair facilities, yet another graving dock was required by the turn of century. Larger ships were planned and the new dock would need to accommodate them. The site chosen was at the western edge of the docks land, and separated from the previous constructions. Work began in January 1900 necessitating the removal of 266,200 cubic yards of spoil to facilitate the dock which was 875 feet long by 90 feet wide and 33 feet deep, at a projected cost of £229,000, consuming some 133,000 cubic yards of concrete. Much of the soil removed was used to reclaim land along the foreshore of the West Bay. The completion of the works in 1905 coincided with the centenary of the battle of Trafalgar and accordingly, the new dock was given the name Trafalgar Dock at its opening ceremony, performed by the Marquis of Winchester on 21st October. The first vessel to make use of this new facility was the Union Castle ship *Dunluce Castle* which entered the dock on 17th November that year.

An early scene during the building of the Trafalgar Drydock. This photograph taken around 1900 shows Aird's men at work on preliminary excavations. The outline of the drydock can be seen on the left while vast expanse in the centre of the photograph would later become the White Star (Ocean) Dock. The South Western Hotel can be seen at the top right behind the timber transit shed, lined with rail wagons, which stands roughly where Central Road is today. The buildings of Queens Terrace are directly ahead in the distance beyond Platform Road. (Bert Moody collection)

VIPs and City dignitaries parade from their train across the entrance gates of the new Trafalgar Drydock on 21st October 1905 in preparation for the opening ceremony performed by the Marquis of Winchester, seen leading the party with Sir Charles Scotter, Chairman of the LSWR. (Bert Moody collection)

The Marquis of Winchester operates the lever to flood the new drydock. The building behind the honoured party is the Trafalgar Dock pumping station. (Bert Moody collection)

The SS Deutschland in the Trafalgar Drydock prior to the dock's enlargement. This was before the building of the White Star Dock and, at the time, berths at 50 and 51 had not been completed, nor had the Harland and Wolff workshops been extended along the western side of the dock.
(Jeff Pain Collection)

Days gone by with the Red Star Line's vessel Finland in the Trafalgar Drydock before the erection of the Harland & Wolff workshops in 1907. The ship was built in 1902 and broken up in 1927. (Bert Moody Collection)

By the time the White Star Dock was nearing completion it was decided the nearly new Trafalgar Dock would need to be enlarged and Topham, Jones & Railton were awarded this additional contract. The dock, being 875 feet long with a 90 feet wide entrance was now inadequate for the White Star Line vessels such as the *Olympic*, then under construction. Ideas for yet another larger drydock had been considered as part of a docks extension at Woolston on the River Itchen and a 1909 drawing shows the drydock outline at Weston Point. Land was purchased in anticipation of the works but several factors rendered the scheme impractical. Firstly, it would have been divorced from the rest of the docks, and a railway connection would mean a lengthy round trip via St Denys on the Netley branch line. There were other issues, such as lack of land for expansion and the building of a new branch line, so the idea was discarded in favour of enlarging the existing Trafalgar Dock, which would be both a quicker and cheaper alternative.

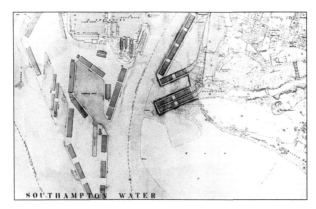

An abandoned plan of the Woolston extension shows the proposed new quays, sheds and railways along the shoreline opposite the existing docks. (Bert Moody Collection)

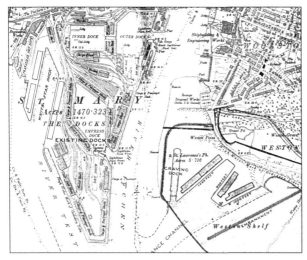

Another scheme showing the proposed works off Weston which included a new drydock and several more quays. Embankment earthworks would have enclosed the site during its construction. (Bert Moody Collection)

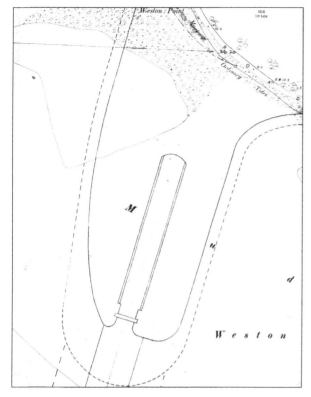

The proposed new drydock at Weston never got off the drawing board. Along with its connecting branch line railway through Woolston it was abandoned in favour of widening the Trafalgar Dock. (Dave Marden Collection)

The alterations began in 1911 and involved the cutting back of the thick concrete walls to widen the dock and increase its length to 897 feet. The entrance also being widened from 90 to 100 feet. At the same time, the entrance gates were replaced by a sliding steel caisson. The work took two years to complete and the newly enlarged dock was re-opened in April 1913.

One final alteration occurred in 1922 when a 'V' shape was cut into the dock head to accommodate the bow of the Cunard vessel *Berengaria*, in effect increasing the dock length by another 15 feet.

Above are two views of work in progress during the enlarging of the Trafalgar drydock in April 1911. The left photograph is looking north towards the Harland and Wolff workshops while, right, the opposite direction looks towards the caisson. (both Jeff Pain Collection)

The White Star Line steamship *Teutonic* gets an overhaul at the Trafalgar Drydock. (Bert Moody Collection)

Like the others before it, the Trafalgar Drydock fell victim to the demise of the British ship repair industry and was out of use in 1989. It was afterwards filled for the greater part with green sand from main channel dredging, and also topped with a surface for vehicle storage. However, part of it which is still exposed at the caisson end is intended to be incorporated into a new aerial and nautical museum.

Left: Looking north to the head of the Trafalgar Drydock after the 15 foot cut out was made.

Right: Looking down on the scene at berth 49 and across to the Trafalgar Drydock, where the *Asturias* is afloat. To the right are the passenger sheds of berth 46 and 47 at the Ocean Dock.

7. The White Star Dock

In 1907 White Star Line transferred their north Atlantic vessels from Liverpool to Southampton and further quays were needed to accommodate them. Contractors Topham, Jones and Railton were engaged to carry out the task of building the White Star Dock (renamed Ocean Dock in 1922) and were awarded a contract in October that year. The 15.5 acre dock, though smaller in area than the Empress dock, was much deeper with a clearance of 40 feet at low water. It boasted 3,807 feet of new quays and was completed in 1911, although various ships were laid up at the new quays before the official opening. The dock was used almost exclusively by White Star, Cunard, and United States Lines but the shorter quay at berth 45 became the domain of timber traffic.

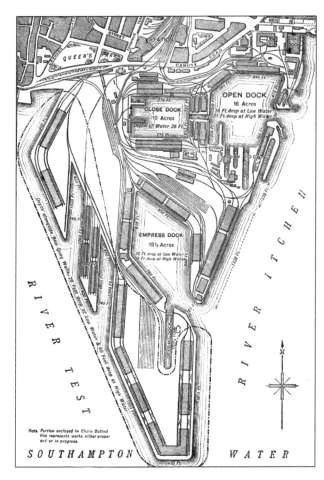

An early plan of the berths along the Test Quays prior to the construction of the Trafalgar Drydock in 1905. It shows two docks which were later redesigned as the larger White Star Dock when built. (Jeff Pain Collection)

Most of the area needed for the dock's development was already contained within the enclosing embankment which had been set up after the construction of the Test Quays and used to facilitate the building of the Trafalgar Drydock. Despite leakage through the chalk embankment, the site had been kept reasonably dry by a drainage system of sumps that were regularly pumped out into the sea. To alleviate this leakage, tongue and grooved wooden piles were driven into its seaward side before work commenced in 1907.

The dock itself would extend beyond the embankment and was built in three stages. Area A, inside the bank, would include berths 43 to 46 and the greater part of berth 47, area B outside the bank, would include the remainder of berth 47, together with berths 48, 49 and 42, while in area C, berth 41 would be built into the bank itself.

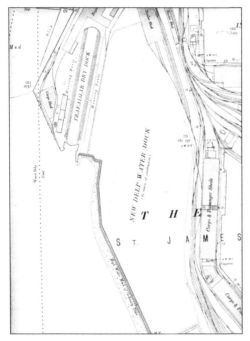

Left: A 1910 drawing shows the enclosing embankment across the site of the New Deep Water Dock (White Star Dock) during the course of its construction. When complete, the scheme provided berths 41 to 49. The Trafalgar Drydock is already in place, as are berths 50 and 51 to the left of it. The sheds on the right are at berths 21-23 serving the Empress Dock. (Dave Marden collection)

Below: A plan of the White Star Dock construction areas A, B & C shows the line of the original enclosing embankment stretching across from berth 41 to 47 and over to the entrance of the Trafalgar Dock.

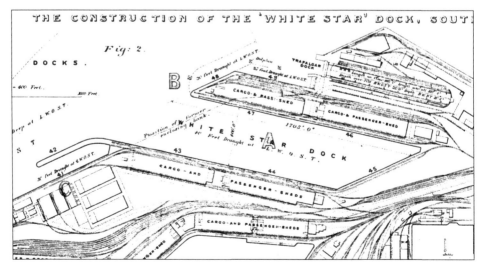

The walls inside the bank (section A) were constructed in concrete with a long toe projecting out from the cope line to stabilise the wall and prevent lateral movement as in earlier dock constructions. The base had a slope of 1 in 8 from front to rear, also to alleviate previous problems. The back of the wall was built in steps to take the weight of the backing material and the wall itself was built in 100 foot sections. The cope was capped in granite and contained a trench for water pipes and electricity cables.

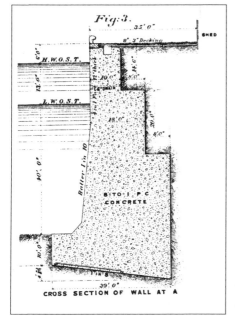

A diagram of the design for the wall used in the greater part of the dock constructed inside the embankment at section A.

The foundation trenches for the walls were relatively trouble free apart from the south end of berth 43 where a couple of 'blow holes' were allowing in water and fine sand, possibly via the porous gravel below the bed of the dock. Sheet piling was erected and reinforced concrete caissons were built to be sunk into the base of the trench. The caissons measured 16 feet 9 inches long by 8 feet 3 inches wide and 16 feet deep. Their walls were 18 inches thick and they each weighed about 62 tons. The caissons were sunk into position in pairs with the added weight of an extra 76 tons, provided by 24 foot sections of rails, stood on end. Once in position, the caissons were filled, then covered, with 12 inches of concrete.

The dry area inside the embankment had been excavated to 30 feet or so below the quay walls with a combination of steam navvies and hand digging by labourers, the spoil being hauled up inclines by rail wagons then mostly tipped into hopper barges and dumped off the Isle of Wight. Totalling 595,000 cubic yards, the material was transported at the rate of 12,000 cubic yards per day, although some of the spoil, about 111,000 cubic yards, was used to reclaim part of the foreshore along the West Bay, as had some of the earlier excavations from the Trafalgar Drydock.

Above and below views show the contractors steam navvies and railways at work on the White Star Dock in 1908. Note the trucks at the centre left of the upper photograph where much of the digging was still being performed manually by gangs of men. (both Dave Marden Collection)

Early works in excavating the White Star Dock in May 1908 show a line of railway wagons laden with soil being hauled away for dumping into barges. (Jeff Pain Collection)

The May 1908 scene viewed from the bottom of the wagon incline where piles and shuttering are made ready for the concrete foundations. (Jeff Pain Collection)

It is now July 1908 and works are in hand behind the enclosing embankment. To the left is a White Star vessel in the Trafalgar Drydock, completed in 1905. (Jeff Pain Collection)

Another view of the White Star Dock in May 1909 shows railway wagons lining the eastern side of the works where the buildings of Harland & Wolff are visible. On the right is the South Western Hotel. (Jeff Pain Collection)

Another photograph from May 1909 shows giant cranes on the temporary jetty at the enclosing embankment. (Jeff Pain Collection)

The railway wagons on the temporary jetty where the excavated soil was tipped into hopper barges for dumping off the Isle of Wight. (Jeff Pain Collection)

The other side of the soil tipping gantry with the barge ramps raised. (Jeff Pain Collection)

Progress was well advanced by February 1910 with the exposed concrete walls of the White Star Dock rising to the quay level. This view looks across berth 45 towards the Empress Dock. (Jeff Pain Collection)

This section of the quay wall construction was at berth 46 in March 1910. The buildings on the left, beyond the crane, are the Harland & Wolff Workshops at the Trafalgar Drydock. (Jeff Pain Collection)

Also in March 1910 the construction of the quay wall at berth 44 was well under way. The cargo sheds in the background are those of berths 20 and 21 at the Empress Dock. (Jeff Pain Collection)

The works at berth 44 viewed from another angle in March 1910 with the South Western Hotel in the right background. (Jeff Pain Collection)

A few months later the quay walls resemble a giant bathtub after the dock had been flooded to enable dredging. This is the corner of berth 45 with berths 46 and 47 stretching out on the right. (Jeff Pain Collection)

Construction of the eastern quay wall in June 1910. This would become berth 43 where the fateful voyage of the RMS *Titanic* began less than two years later. (Jeff Pain Collection)

Another photograph taken in June 1910 shows water being pumped from the trenches behind the quay walls. Much of the enclosing embankment on the left of the picture was still in place after the dock had been flooded. (Jeff Pain Collection)

The date is now April 1911 and work is in progress on the quay wall at berth 47. (Jeff Pain Collection)

Another view of the giant cranes on the embankment temporary jetty, this time in April 1911. (Jeff Pain Collection)

Looking across the rubble of the nearly completed White Star Dock in April 1911 from the corner of berths 45 and 46. The passenger sheds at berths 43 and 44 on the far side are almost complete. (Jeff pain Collection)

Work is forging ahead in June 1911 and berths 43/4, on the far side of the dock, are ready for the arrival of the new White Star Line ship *Olympic* for her maiden voyage on the 14th of that month. On the near side of the dock at berth 46 is the Union Castle Liner *Carisbrooke Castle*. (Dave Marden Collection)

A photograph of the White Star Dock taken from the roof of the South Western Hotel shows the 'almost new' passenger sheds on the right at berths 46 and 47. (Jeff Pain Collection)

By April 1910 the walls in area A were almost complete and the area inside the embankment now needed to be dredged to a depth of 40 feet below low water. A passage was cut through the embankment to flood the dock and allow in dredgers to perform the task, which was carried out by the contractor's three dredgers, two tugs, eight steam hoppers, and five dumb hoppers. These were assisted by the railway company's own dredger *Waterloo* with an additional three steam hoppers.

Section B of the dock construction was carried out in the open water outside of the embankment. The foundation trenches with timber sheet piling were dug for the quay walls at berths 47 to 49 with the help of divers. A concrete base was laid with a similar 1 in 8 slope from front to back while the front and back of the walls were faced with concrete blocks weighing between 6 and 8 tons and in-filled with concrete during dry spells between tides. Part of the backing material was of broken concrete obtained from the widening of the adjacent Trafalgar Drydock.

The concrete blocks were made from moulds in a yard set up between berth 46 and the Trafalgar Dock where a pair of stationary mixers deposited the material into small tip wagons running on an elevated railway. When set, the blocks were stacked at the south end of the yard, then transported by narrow gauge railway to the wall.

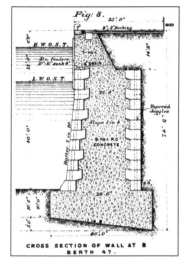

A cross section of the wall at B, built in the open water at berth 47 outside the embankment shows the difference from the design used for the enclosed section A.

The timber jetty at berth 42 was originally designed as a cattle dock and a third of it was already in place by the time the White Star works had begun, but it would now serve several purposes. Firstly, it would act as a guiding stage for ships entering and leaving the dock, while also providing a working or lay-up berth. The latter construction consisted of a similar design with 16 inch square piles driven in five rows, braced by 2 inch diameter iron ties. These were strengthened by concrete buttresses at regular intervals and topped by decking timbers of 9 x 3 inches.

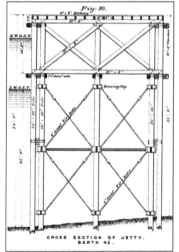

The jetty at berth 42 showing its construction of timber piles and iron tie rods.

The final stage of the White Star Dock scheme was the building of berth 41, sited within the enclosing embankment. This was quite different from the previous designs and consisted of concrete piers and arches with curtain walls. Trenches were sunk down through the bank into the natural surface below it and sheet piling applied to the area above. The toe of the wall was less pronounced than on the other walls and the whole construction was supported at its rear by a reinforced concrete platform on piles set at 10 feet 6 inches below the quay level. The weight above it was made up with ashes, counter balancing the load on the wall itself.

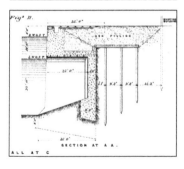

A cross section of the pier and arch design for the quay wall at berth 41 which was built into the enclosing embankment. The reinforced concrete platform behind, topped with ashes, acted as a counter balance to the wall itself.

The scene during construction of the knuckle at berth 41 at the entrance to the White Star Dock with the spoil tipping jetty on the right. The International Cold Storage and Ice Company building is seen at berth 40 where the two pillars appear to be shafts housing lifts or hoists to the upper floors. (Jeff Pain Collection)

Further works in hand on the Test Quay looking north in June 1910. (Jeff Pain Collection)

A photograph from around 1930 shows a vessel discharging timber at berth 41. The timber jetty on the right provided an additional berth No.42. (Bert Moody Collection)

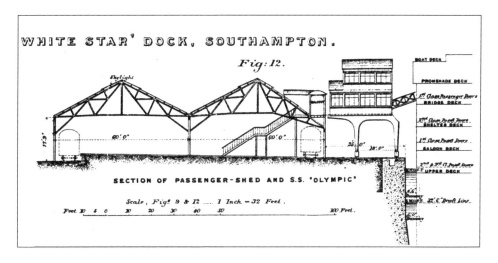

A cross section of the quay at berths 43/4 shows the position of the travelling passenger gangway towers linking the *Olympic* with the shed's upper passenger walkways.

Owing to the extreme height of new liners such as White Star's *Olympic*, travelling passenger towers were provided at berths 43/4 to transfer passengers from the upper decks to the reception sheds. (Dave Marden Collection)

American Line vessels *St Louis* and *Philadelphia* along with White Star Line's *Majestic* in the White Star Dock viewed from the *Titanic* on 10th April 1912. (Dave Marden collection)

A busy Ocean Dock in the early 1920s shows Cunard's *Mauretania* and *Aquitania* at berths 46 and 47 with possibly a White Star Line ship at berth 43 and an American Line vessel at berth 44. (Jeff Pain Collection)

Lots of activity in this view of Central Road, adjacent to the White Star Dock around 1930, with the bow of a liner visible on the left at 44 berth while a passenger train approaches the terminal from the right. (Jeff Pain Collection)

The timber storage shed at berth 45 shortly after construction around 1930. (Bert Moody Collection)

Several new passenger terminals were added or refurbished from existing buildings over the years following nationalisation of the docks in 1948. The Ocean Terminal replaced the old transit sheds at berths 43/44 when it was opened in 1950. Work had begun in December 1946 and was completed on 31st July 1950, when it was officially opened by Prime Minister Clement Atlee. The new terminal was used for the first time on the following day by Cunard's *Queen Elizabeth*. Sadly, with the steady decline in passengers who had taken to air travel, the building gradually fell into disuse. Having been used on a few occasions for exhibitions the outmoded building finally succumbed to demolition in 1983.

A post-Second World War scene with the Ocean Dock well occupied. The Town Quay is visible at the top left. (Jeff Pain Collection)

After the austere post-war period, redevelopment of the docks saw the prodigious new Ocean Terminal rise alongside berths 43/44. Here it is nearing completion on 26th March 1950. (Bert Moody Collection)

Mobile cranes lift a concrete section of the pedestrian footbridge across Ocean Road. This will carry visitors up to the viewing gallery at the new Ocean Terminal.

The newly completed Ocean Terminal awaits its official opening. This photograph taken about April 1950 shows the *Queen Mary* on the opposite side of the dock at berths 46/7. The Inner and Outer docks are at the top of the picture with the Empress Dock on the right. (Dave Marden Collection)

To commemorate the opening of their new Ocean Terminal, the British Transport Commission produced an eight page brochure exhorting the unequalled facilities on offer at the new building with ground floor platforms for boat trains and sumptuous first floor lounges that even included an 'iced water fountain'. (Dave Marden Collection)

The sleek 'modern' lines of the Ocean Terminal, with its gleaming white concrete facade, ushers in the post-war period of the Eastern Docks renaissance. (Jeff Pain Collection)

One of the Ocean Terminal's swish Art Deco lounges oozes opulence and comfort with its luxurious leather furnishings. (Jeff Pain Collection)

The glory days of the Ocean Dock were fast fading into history when this photo was taken in the summer of 1982. The Ocean Terminal was obsolete, with berths 43/44 occupied by the laid-up bulk tanker *Tantalus* and the passenger sheds opposite had been demolished for the building of a new grain terminal. (Bert Moody Collection)

The Ocean Dock suffered something of a decline with its glory days of transatlantic liners fading into history. The once celebrated berths became home to laid-up vessels, a scrapyard, and a grain terminal but, with the revival of the cruise trade, it is once again welcoming passengers. A new Ocean Terminal opened in April 2009, but is now at berth 46/47 on the opposite side of the Ocean Dock from its illustrious former namesake.

8. Berths 48-51

The quays at berths 50 and 51 were built around the time the Trafalgar Drydock was constructed and then widened. Berths 48 and 49 were built along with the White Star Dock and were primarily used for the lay up of vessels undergoing repair, either in the drydock itself or at the adjacent quays, although there was a cargo shed at berth 50 which was replaced by a flying boat terminal in 1948. There was also a small railway station at the corner of berths 50-51 where passengers would board tenders that carried them off to ships lying in Southampton Water or Cowes Roads.

In later years berth 48 became the home base of the 150 ton capacity Floating Crane which, after its introduction on 11th November 1924, became a towering feature of the port, visible from distance by land or sea. It was used for heavy lifts, not only in the docks, but also performed many other tasks around the port. Having no propulsion system of its own it was always moved with the accompaniment of tugs. After 60 years of sterling work it was replaced by a more modern type with a greater lifting capacity of 200 tonnes.

Above: The 150 ton capacity Floating Crane moored in its customary position at berth 48. (Dave Marden)

One of the many tasks called upon the Floating Crane was the transfer of Southern Railway stock to the Isle of Wight. Here, a consignment of passenger coaches makes the trip in 1938.

The *Empire Windrush* sits at berth 49 on 29th March 1950 with the *Queen Mary* occupying berth 46/7 in the Ocean Dock. (Bert Moody Collection)

The last major phase of the Eastern Docks construction was the arrival of the Floating Drydock in 1924. Having been built on the Tyne by the firm of Armstrong Whitworth it was towed to Southampton and installed at berth 50 where it was officially declared open on 12th July 1924 by the Prince of Wales (later Edward VIII) aboard the paddle steamer *Duchess of Fife* which sailed through the submerged dock. The Union Castle liner *Arundel Castle* was then installed to demonstrate its workings. With an overall length of 960 feet and a width of 134 feet it had side walls some 70 feet high. To enable its lowering when receiving vessels for repair it was necessary to dredge the seabed below to a depth of 65 feet. The dock provided a much needed facility until the completion of the King George V Graving Dock in 1933 as part of the New Docks Extension, after which it was little used.

The Floating Drydock under tow on its way to Southampton in 1924.

The floating dock in position at berth 50 with the White Star Line *Olympic* in the background. (Dave Marden Collection)

An excellent view of White Star Line's *Olympic* in the floating drydock. The Hythe Ferry is passing at the bottom right and passengers would certainly have been afforded spectacular views. (Dave Marden Collection)

Having been out of regular use since 1934, the floating drydock gained a new lease of life and eventually suffered a dramatic finale. It was sold to the Admiralty in 1939-40 and moved to Portsmouth, being renamed *AFD No.11*, remaining there until acquired by the Rotterdam Dock Company in 1959 where it was employed until the company went out of business in 1983. New Brazilian owners purchased the drydock, but while under tow off the coast of Spain it was lost in a storm. The structure was transported in two sections, each placed on pontoons, when one broke away and was wrecked on the Spanish coast while the other was taken into Vigo and later scrapped.

In the meantime berth 50, disused since the departure of the floating drydock, was redeveloped as a Marine Air Terminal from where the British Overseas Aircraft Corporation (BOAC) inaugurated flights to Madeira on 14th April 1948, with later links to Lisbon and Las Palmas. The services ended on 3rd November 1950 when BOAC abandoned flying boats and pulled out of Southampton. However, the service was taken over by Aquila Airways, who had been in existence since July 1948, and had previously purchased a number of flying boats from BOAC.

The newly opened Marine Air Terminal at berth 50 in 1948 showing the pontoon cradles where passengers embarked. The Trafalgar drydock is at the rear with the Harland & Wolff workshops at its head.

BOAC flying boat *Southampton* alongside the Marine Air Terminal with the Town Quay in the background. The aircraft was named on 14th April 1948 by the Mayor of Southampton at the inauguration of the new terminal which had replaced the former floating drydock.

Madeira was often a destination for winter sun and an advertisement for Aquila Airways in 1951 offers an incredible 26 per cent reduction in off-season fares from May to November. (Dave Marden Collection)

They took up the regular service from Southampton to Madeira and also operated charter flights to such places as Goa, Helsinki, Karachi, Malta and Lake Garda, but with the competition of faster jet aircraft, and the high maintenance cost of their ageing craft, they ceased operations after the Solent flying boat *Awatere* took off for Madeira on 26th September 1958 and returned four days later.

A seemingly disinterested young lady is oblivious to the nearby Aquila Airways flying boat in the mid 1950s. (Dave Mines)

The terminal became the shore base of *HMS Wessex* and in 1964 was occupied by the Royal Naval Reserve, which had previously been aboard a vessel of that name moored at berth 14 in the Inner Dock. After the RNR unit had closed in 1994 the building was finally taken down in 1996.

The final layout of the Old (Eastern) Docks showing the various quays, basins and drydocks. (Dave Marden Collection)

Part Two – The West Bay preparations

9. The Town Quay & Royal Pier

The Town Quay and Royal Pier were never part of the docks estate until an amalgamation with the dock owners came about in 1968. Prior to that they were administered firstly, from 1803, by the Harbour Commissioners and latterly by the Southampton Harbour Board. The Town Quay was little more than a stone jetty in its early days and from 1853 underwent several rebuilds and improvements to its length to accommodate the increasing size of ships but it was always limited to coastal and near-continental vessels. The Victoria (Royal) Pier was first constructed in 1833 and substantially enlarged in 1892 when the original wooden structure was doubled in width and lengthened to include a pavilion, tea rooms and a bandstand. A railway from the Docks (Terminus) Station served both the quay and pier – the latter even having its own railway station until the First World War.

Looking south at the entrance to the Royal Pier after the 1892 rebuild.
(Jeff Pain Collection)

The view north from the Royal Pier in its heyday, packed with trippers and promenaders showing the pavilion on the right. (Jeff Pain Collection)

The Royal Pier railway station was still in regular use when this turn of the century photograph was taken. The building on the extreme right was originally a club house for a local yacht club but the leisure steamer booking offices around it quickly became attached. (Jeff Pain Collection)

The ferry from Hythe Pier ran to the Town Quay from 1880 and is still in operation today. This pre-1925 view shows the old Harbour Board offices beyond the vessel's funnel. (Jeff Pain Collection)

The seafront at the Town Quay in less hectic days shows the new 1925 built Harbour Board offices on the left while nearby, a hansom cab stands at the Hythe Ferry landing. An ice cream seller pedals his tricycle at the bottom left. (Jeff Pain Collection)

A view from the Town Quay itself showing the old Harbour Board works yard on the right. (Jeff Pain Collection)

With the grouping of the railway companies in 1923, the Southern Railway became owner of Southampton Docks and, like its predecessor, the LSWR, saw the potential revenues from large scale investment.

Southampton Corporation had plans of their own to develop the West Bay but were hampered by finance – not so the Southern Railway who took up the idea and brought about one of the biggest changes the town had seen with the reclamation of over 400 acres of tidal mud, providing new quays, another drydock and a huge new area for industrial redevelopment.

Some reclamation along the shore had already taken place prior to the building of the Pirelli factory in 1912, using spoil from the building of the Trafalgar Drydock, and a railway from the West Station to a train ferry jetty near the Royal Pier had been built by the military in 1917 to supply troops across the Channel on the Western Front but this was largely abandoned when hostilities ceased. Although much of the derelict track had been lifted by the 1920s the ferry jetty itself remained and was incorporated into the scheme.

Initial works in early 1927 saw the widening of the bottleneck frontage along the Town Quay and Royal Pier where trams, commercial vehicles and railway freight competed for space. The alterations were needed to allow for the huge increase in traffic of both road and rail that would be necessary once the works commenced. Part of the area between the Town Quay and Royal Pier was reclaimed from the sea. Here the roadway was widened and new railway lines laid in to carry the vast amounts of materials required during the new dock construction, these connected to the main line at the Terminus Station via the Old (Eastern) Docks tracks. One of the 'casualties' of these works was the existing Royal Pier entrance building, erected when the pier was rebuilt in 1892, but now to be replaced by a more 'modern' structure further back on the pier itself.

Shipping at the Town Quay waned in the 1970s and the warehouses and workshops were replaced by commercial and retail developments in the 1990s. The Royal Pier had been in decline by the time of the docks amalgamation and but a series of fires in 1987 and 1992 signalled its end and eventual closure, and only the rusting ironwork remains in place. However, the 1930 entrance building still stands and is in current use as a restaurant.

The scene in February 1927 before works commenced shows the original quayside wall between the Town Quay and Royal Pier with its old entrance building in the centre of the picture. The former military train ferry jetty can be seen in the distance. (Tony Chilcott Collection)

Preparatory piling work near the Royal Pier in March 1927 ahead of constructing a new outfall pipe. In the centre of the photograph can be seen the buildings of the Royal Southampton Yacht Club, the Wool House, and Royal Pier Hotel. The latter was destroyed by an air raid in the Second World War. (Tony Chilcott Collection)

Dredged material being deposited between the Town Quay and Royal Pier in March 1927. The former Sun Hotel is on the left of the picture at the bottom of the High Street. Behind the domed Harbour Board building stands the Parsons Engineering works while the funnels of a Cunard liner in the distant Ocean Dock can be seen. (Tony Chilcott Collection)

The same scene looking ashore towards the old Harbour Board warehouses opposite the quayside. To the right is Seaway House, which, along with the largest of the warehouses, still survives today. (Tony Chilcott Collection)

A busy scene at the Town Quay shows the reclamation work was well under way by 15th June 1927. (Tony Chilcott Collection)

Trams, trains, and trucks compete for space at the congested Town Quay seafront, viewed from the bottom of the High Street.

The same scene after the road and rail widening works had been completed. Note the skeletal dome of the new Royal Pier entrance building taking shape around April 1929. (both Tony Chilcott Collection)

17-12-28

The steelwork frame for the new Royal Pier entrance building dome begins to take shape on 17th December 1928. (Tony Chilcott Collection)

Three days later and the skeleton of the new entrance building is almost complete. The clock tower of its predecessor is visible in the distance to the left of the dome. (Tony Chilcott Collection)

It is 25th May 1929 and the new Royal Pier entrance building is well advanced with the dome almost complete. (Tony Chilcott Collection)

Another view of the new entrance building, this time looking west towards what will eventually become Mayflower Park. (Tony Chilcott Collection)

On a wet November day in 1929 the former Royal Pier entrance building stands condemned with its replacement now in place. Soon, the railway to the new docks will run through the site the old building occupies. (Tony Chilcott Collection)

Reclamation of the bay was divided into four stages, the first, consisting of 16 acres, including the creation of a 10 acre site for the various contractors materials to be stored, and for the location of a large concrete mixing plant. This area would eventually be cleared, levelled and handed over by the Southern Railway to the Town Corporation as a recreation area, now known as Mayflower Park.

Before these works could begin, a 24-inch diameter cast-iron drainage pipeline was laid along the shore wall from the West Quay to an outfall near the Royal Pier. This would soon be superseded by something on a much grander scale as the plan unfolded. The greater area of the bay would be reclaimed in two stages as works progressed on the enclosing quay wall, while the final stage would be the building of the drydock at Millbrook.

The 24-inch cast-iron drainage pipeline being attached to the sea wall along Western Esplanade prior to the reclamation works. A horse-drawn wagon heads westwards past the Mayflower memorial towards the Royal Pier in March 1927. (Tony Chilcott Collection)

A comparison with the previous photograph shows the construction area had been fenced off by 17th May 1927. (Tony Chilcott Collection)

The banking machine *Bankwell* deposits dredged material ashore between the Royal Pier and the former train ferry jetty seen in the background on 10th May 1927. (Tony Chilcott Collection)

Work progressing on the first docks reclamation area during May 1927 with construction of the new sea wall that will contain the area for the contractors' yard and cement plant. In the background is the former train ferry jetty. This site was later to become Mayflower Park. (Tony Chilcott Collection)

The obsolete First World War train ferry jetty was brought back into service and is shown in 1928 supporting a pipeline from the vessel *Riparian*. (Tony Chilcott Collection)

Part of the reclamation area facing the old Corporation Yard on the shoreline at Western Esplanade in 1928. (Tony Chilcott Collection)

By February 1928 the first part of the docks reclamation was nearing completion and the sea wall of what will become Mayflower Park takes on a familiar shape. The fencing closes off public access from the Royal Pier, where the tall funnels of the Isle of Wight paddlers await their duties. (Tony Chilcott Collection)

10. Preparations along the Western Shore

Buildings along the shoreline around West Bay from Southampton West (now Southampton Central) railway station to the Royal Pier included those of the old electricity power station, the town baths, the Pirelli Cable Works, a corporation yard and a few huddled boatyards. Although high tide afforded pleasant views across the bay, normally the vista was a desolate expanse of mud, occasionally covered by water to allow in the odd shallow drafted vessel. The power station originally had its own pier to bring in coal by barge, but this was abandoned in favour of a rail link joining the main line just east of the West Station. The electricity power station had a cooling pond with an intake and outflow on the shore. Pirelli's had a small jetty which appears to have fallen out of use by the time the new docks scheme came into being. There were also several storm water and drainage outfalls running into the bay but during exceptional tides in spring and autumn, these also allowed the sea to flow in and cause local flooding.

The shore along the West Bay before reclamation with terraced houses and the Temperance Hotel in the centre of the picture. Southampton West railway station clock tower can be seen in the distance. (Dave Marden Collection)

As work progressed the old shoreline would disappear and a major scheme began in 1928 to lay in culverts that would carry the previous drainage and storm water outflows to the new quayside. Firstly, the shoreline was widened along its entire length by the depositing of chalk from the Southern Railway's quarry at Micheldever and, into this, a series of 7-foot diameter concrete pipes were laid in a trench that ran from an outfall at Southampton West station and also accommodated the intake and outflows of the Electricity Power Station cooling pond, together with several other outfalls along the route. The pipes from the power station were installed first, with the main culvert above them, forming a shamrock design which was then embedded in concrete.

The culverting work was carried out by contractors Charles Brand and Son and saw the storm water pipe terminate at a new pumping station at what is now berth 101, while those from the power station exited at the western end of the construction yard (now Mayflower Park). The 54-inch diameter high-voltage pumps at the station are still called upon when storm conditions prevail in the lower town.

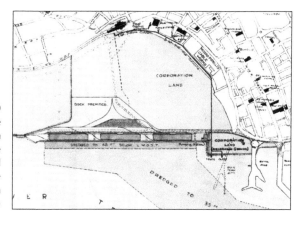

A drawing from January 1930 showing the progress of the New Docks construction with the position of the culverts around the bay and their terminal points at the new quays. (Dave Marden Collection)

One of the outfalls to be culverted was the Shirley Outlet which ran under the west end of Southampton West (Central) Railway station, seen here with assorted rubbish in April 1928.

The first section of chalk filling of the foreshore near the Southampton West Station which is seen centre right of this picture taken in May 1928.

The jetty at the Pirelli works had become something of a dumping ground for waste material by May 1928.

A section of the 7 foot diameter concrete culvert that would carry water and drainage to the new pumping station at berth 101. The word 'Brick' on the right is part of the Brickwood Ales sign on the Royal Standard public house.

More of the pipe sections assembled off the Western Esplanade on 4th July 1928. The Pirelli works are in the centre background.

By June 1928 culvert laying was well under way with the back filling of the trench near the Southampton West Station.

Further progress as the trenching excavations commence south of the Pirelli works in December 1928.

The culvert pipes in place on 19th June 1928.

Culvert works in progress near the Pirelli works in June 1929 as the contractor's locomotive lends a hand.

August 1929 saw the building of box dams at the intake and outlet (nearest) connections of the power station pond to the culverts.

Looking south from the power station towards the Pirelli works, this may appear to be a winter snow scene but the date is August 1929 with tons of chalk having been deposited along the shoreline.

It is now August 1930 looking south past the Pirelli works where the general scene of clutter hides the completion of the triple culvert at this point.

The new pumping station stands ready on the quayside at berth 101 in April 1931. In the foreground is one of the concrete monoliths from which the new quays were constructed. A similar pumping facility was incorporated into the building of the King George V Drydock at the other end of the bay.

Part Three – The Western Docks

11. Reclamation and The New (Western) Docks

Whereas all the previous docks built at Southampton had been basins gouged from the seabed, the new extension would be the result of reclamation and would convert over 400 acres of West Bay mudlands into usable land. Of this, 116 acres at the eastern end were given over to Southampton Corporation and the 10 acre contractor's site became Mayflower Park. At the western end was to be another monster drydock and, as with all its predecessors in their time, it would again be the biggest in the world. The method of infilling was achieved by dredged material taken from the potential main shipping channel and then being liquidised by seawater before being pumped ashore via 2 foot diameter pipes. This task was undertaken by the James Contracting and Dredging Company, who had been long established in the port.

The new quays, of around one and a half miles in length, were built along a straight enclosing embankment, constructed of gravel taken from the dredging. It was some 167 feet wide and stretched for almost two miles across the bay between the Royal Pier and Millbrook Point. A line of 146 concrete monoliths, each weighing 5,000 tons with V-shaped steel 'shoes', were sunk along its course at depths up to 100 feet below quay level. The monoliths were 45 feet square and each had nine 10 feet wide octagonal wells through which material could be extracted during the course of their sinking. In some cases, the added weight of up to 4,000 tons of cast-iron blocks was required to assist the operation. When the monolith reached its required depth the wells were part-filled with 15 feet of concrete, then sand or soil was added to the rear three and water to the other six. Their tops were afterwards covered with concrete slabs. As with earlier quay constructions, a void was created behind the new sea wall to relieve pressure, this gap being covered by concrete slabs with dimensions 38 feet long, eight feet wide and four feet thick.

The quay wall itself was built of concrete, rising above the monoliths which were then covered with six feet of gravel as a bed for the railway tracks, with the top surface being of reinforced concrete and tarmac. Concrete walls supporting the quayside crane tracks were laid directly onto the monoliths for strength and stability.

The main contractor for the New Docks was Sir Robert McAlpine & Sons (London) Ltd and much of the work was performed by versatile Smith's cranes of 5 and 7 ton capacity. Over 20 of these, steam operated on standard gauge railway tracks, created the forest of jibs seen in many photographs. As with previous constructions at Southampton docks, railways and locomotives were used to transport heavy materials around the site. McAlpines had their own fleet of engines and at least 19 were involved in the works.

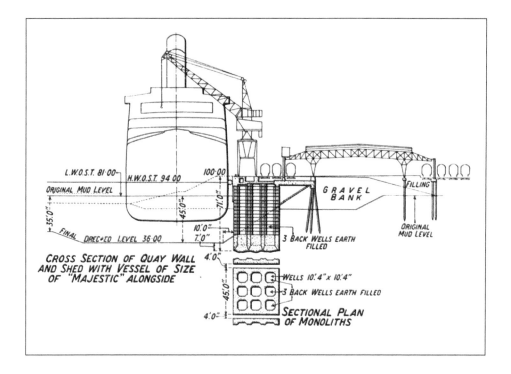

The above diagram shows a cross section of the quay construction illustrating the original level of mud in the bay, the gravel bank and the position of the concrete monoliths. The plan of the monoliths shows the octagonal shafts, or wells, that were filled to stabilise them. (Dave Marden Collection)

Concrete blocks were inserted into the monoliths to form the octagonal wells. Smiles and overcoats all round as VIPs celebrate the first block being set into No.3 monolith on 5th February 1929.

The scene on 7th February 1929 as the first monoliths are sunk into place.

The main reclamation of the bay was carried out in two phases. As the construction of the new quays spread westwards across the bay, a cross embankment was built out from the shoreline to meet it, roughly dissecting the bay in half. The first section was 177 acres and the second around 165. The area was then in-filled with liquefied dredging material which was raised to a level of 10 feet above the original sea bed. Sluice gates were constructed at the seaward end of the partition embankment to let water run out at low tide and allow the reclaimed area to gradually solidify. The gates were then closed again to keep out the returning tide.

The cross embankment under construction on 6th August 1929. The wooden jetty was reinforced with chalk from Southern Railway's quarry at Micheldever. (Tony Chilcott Collection)

This classic photograph of the West Bay showing the New Docks construction was taken in summer 1929 and contains many interesting features. As construction of the new berths moves across the bay, the cross bank from the shore reaches out to meet it. In the foreground is the main contractor's area (later Mayflower Park) with its concrete mixing plant ashore of the former train ferry jetty. At the bottom is the Royal Pier with both old and new entrance buildings just discernible. The other small jetty on the corner of the site was for the dumping of spoil into barges. The far right shows the initial shore reclamations for the laying of culverts from the power station and the Southampton West railway station further on.

Looking eastwards, the first area of West Bay is enclosed by the cross bank showing the sluice gates where it meets the new quay embankment. In the distance, the Old (Eastern) Docks are busy with liners.

A closer view of the sluice gates for draining the first section of West Bay after the reclamation had commenced. The chimneys of the old power station can be seen on the distant shoreline.

It is now 2nd November 1929 and the line of monoliths stretches across the bay waiting to be sunk into the embankment.

A closer view of the monoliths in place on 4th November 1929.

Cast-iron blocks are heaped upon a monolith to assist its sinking into the embankment.

Work is progressing on 13th January 1930 with the Smith's cranes hard at work along the embankment while, on the right of the photograph, the skeleton of the Stormwater Pumping Station is prominent. (Tony Chilcott Collection)

The dredger *Foremost Chief* pumping sludge ashore from a barge on 17th January 1931. The new quay line is in place with the monoliths capped with concrete slabs.

The other end of the pipeline as the sludge pours into the bay on 6th December 1930. (Tony Chilcott Collection)

The former train ferry jetty had been out of use since the end of the First World War but was returned to active service for vessels discharging cement for the adjacent concrete mixing plant. Seen here on 26th February 1930.

Below: Mobile gantries assisted the placing of heavy materials along the site. Health and Safety regulations weren't quite so prolific on 17th January 1931.

The new quay wall is in place on 15th November 1931, complete with bollards and crane rails and the Stormwater Pumping Station can be seen in the centre distance.

Work progresses on the open quayside as the walls of 101 shed begin to rise on 28th February 1932.

The initial concrete columns and brickwork at berth 101 shed on 1st March 1932.

The view from 'inside' 101 shed, looking eastwards on 4th April 1932. The north wall is complete and the first roof span is in place.

The 101 berth transit shed was almost completed by 23rd July 1932 as this photograph looking west reveals.

Laying the 101 berth shed floor on 22nd September 1932.

Left and below: A dredger and barges lie alongside the new quay as the transit sheds take shape in 1932.

The waiting hall buffet at berths 101/2 was a picture of elegance when first furnished in 1932.

A murky autumn day as the Cunard White Star liner *Mauretania* becomes the first vessel to use the new quays on 19th October 1932 in preparation for her winter lay up. The general debris in the foreground is the corner of the contractor's yard. (Dave Marden Collection)

A view of the 103/4 berth terminal, looking west, on 19th January 1934.

Also on 19th January 1934 this photograph of 103 shed from the sea shows work in hand at Ranks Flour Mills.

An aerial photograph of the works at 103 shed on 19th January reveals the reclaimed West Bay beyond it was still very 'liquid'.

Looking west through 103 berth shed on 2nd March 1934.

Possibly the world's most expensive bicycle rack as the New Docks quays near completion on 8th March 1934. The pumping station for the newly built King George V Drydock looms in the distance.

Work had progressed at berths 103/4 by 11th April 1934 where this photograph shows the completed 103 shed (right centre) and the waiting hall section.

The western end of 104 shed receiving its roof on 4th May 1934.

Looking east along the embankment the first new quays and transit sheds are in place as a dredger pumps sludge into the bay. The four funnelled vessel alongside is the *Mauretania,* which was the first ship to use the new quays.

The construction of the New Docks Sheds is relentless with works on 105 shed surging ahead on 23rd November 1934.

The roofless shed at berth 107 looking east on 23rd November 1934.

The western end of 108 berth transit shed marked the end of the New Docks passenger terminal buildings, seen on 4th April 1935.

The first berths of the New Docks were opened for shipping long before the scheme was completed in 1934. The first two passenger sheds (101/2) were completed by 1932 and the initial vessel, the Cunard White Star Liner *Mauretania* came alongside on 19th October that year for her winter lay up. The sheds were built in pairs, with a central mezzanine waiting hall serving the two. In all, eight sheds were erected in four pairs.

Following reclamation, the vast area behind the quayside sheds, which was previously West Bay, was then developed as an industrial estate with many large factories being established in the ensuing years. The biggest of these belonged to Ranks Flour Mills, Standard Telephones and Cables Ltd, the A.C. Delco division of General Motors and Montague Meyer timber merchants.

Steelwork in place for the floor of Ranks Flour Mill on 14th March 1933.

The completed Ranks Flour Mill on 22nd February 1934 with Dock Gate No.10 to the left of the photograph. The snaking dock boundary fence forms a barrier to the undeveloped sea of dried mud beyond.

Another view of the newly built Ranks Mill looking south towards the River Test with Dock Gate No.10 in the foreground. The first of the two gantries to carry grain from the quayside vessels stretches out to berth 102/103.

Looking back along the gantry towards Ranks Mill on 22nd February 1934.

One of the longest buildings on the reclaimed land of the New Docks estate was the Carriage Cleaning Shed where whole boat trains were made up and heated for the comfort of ship's passengers. The trains, when ready, were moved to transit sheds all over the Old and New Docks to afford passengers a smooth seamless journey to London and beyond. The shed could accommodate six complete trains and had offices and messrooms for the railway company workforce, together with fuelling facilities for the locomotives.

A pair of huge pile-driving towers in preparation for the construction of the Carriage Cleaning Shed on 4th June 1935.

A southern aspect of the Carriage Shed site, also on 4th June 1935 shows the liner *Empress of Britain* at berths 103/4.

The western end of the finished Carriage Shed on 2nd January 1936.

The open eastern entrance to the Carriage Shed on 2nd January 1936 showing the six tracks for the passenger trains.

Inside the Carriage Shed, again on 2nd January 1936, as a B4 class dock shunter tests the internal track with a train of passenger stock.

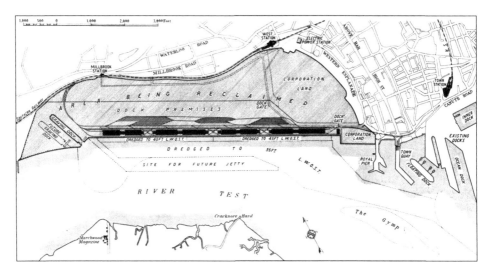

Although the huge docks extension scheme provided many new berths, and the world's largest drydock, plans were already in hand for a further expansion with a new jetty and an additional drydock, but those plans stayed on the drawing board and no further accommodation was built until the first container berths appeared in 1968. (Dave Marden Collection)

A busy scene at the eastern end of the New Docks with the contractors yard on the left and the reclaimed area on the right. The site entrance gate is just to the right of the Mayflower memorial and the two-storey building just inside is the James Dredging Company offices. A works personnel train headed by the now-preserved locomotive T9 class No.120 trundles towards the Eastern Docks via the Town Quay. (Jeff Pain Collection)

The beginnings of Herbert Walker Avenue (named after the Southern Railway General Manager) with the Mayflower memorial in the distance. The paraphernalia of the contractor's yard stretches out on the right of the photograph with the new Royal Pier entrance building beyond. (Tony Chilcott Collection)

Construction works were co-ordinated from the Docks Engineers offices near No.8 gate. This 'temporary' site office building, shown on 31st July 1931, was still in place until quite recent years before its final removal. (Tony Chilcott Collection)

Another view along the beginnings of Herbert Walker Avenue reveals workmen's mess huts and several abandoned wheelbarrows – perhaps it was time for a tea break?

Work is now progressing well in laying the roadway along Herbert Walker Avenue as a contractor's locomotive steams by. (Dave Marden Collection)

Apart from the main construction of the New Docks, several ancillary works were carried out. One of these was to build a new road access into the dock to replace the level crossing at the eastern end of Southampton West Railway Station. The road was built over a viaduct at the western end of the station. Now known as Central Station Bridge it carries traffic via Solent Road to No.10 Gate.

A photograph of works taking place during the building of the Central Station Bridge shows a train with a McAlpine contractor's engine and Southern Railway wagons on 10th May 1934. (Russell Wear Collection/Industrial Locomotive Society)

An advertisement for Smith's Cranes at the time of the constructions at Southampton. The photograph shows early works at the King George V Drydock. (Dave Marden Collection)

Left: An advertisement for Sir Robert McAlpine and Sons for the construction of the New Docks and quayside sheds.

Below: A photograph taken on 22nd August 1936 shows the first occasion when all the New Docks berths were filled. From the right, the vessels are *Empress of Britain*, *Europa*, *Montrose*, *Orontes*, *Strathmore*, *Bencruachen*, *Bellerophon* and *Majestic*. (Bert Moody Collection)

The coaster *Berent* discharging grain via the Rank Hovis conveyors at berth 102 in the New Docks. The vessel behind is one of the Orient Line ships, possibly the *Oronsay*. (Jeff Pain Collection)

A full complement of vessels at the Western Docks quays photographed in 1960 with the United States line's *United States* at berth 107/8 nearest the camera. At the top of the picture there is the troopship *Nevasa* at 101 berth, then come three Union Castle Line vessels *Pretoria Castle, Stirling Castle* and *Pendennis Castle* with an unidentified freighter completing the line up.

Another impressive line up of ships in the Western Docks, this time on 21st January 1963, shows from right to left, *Orsova, Pretoria Castle, Thistleroy, Windsor Castle, Canberra, Oriana, Himalaya* and the GPO cable ship *Monarch*.

Many of the original quayside sheds and terminals at the Western Docks were victims of air raids in the Second World War and have been replaced over the years. The transit shed at berth 102 had suffered severe damage and was reconstructed as a terminal for the Union Castle Line vessels, which then transferred from the Eastern Docks. The building was officially opened on 25th January 1956 by the South African High Commissioner, with the *Edinburgh Castle* being the first ship to call.

The replacement terminal at berth 102 when newly built in 1956 for the Union Castle Line services.

Following the cessation of the South African services in September 1977 the building was incorporated into the Free Trade Zone established at berth 101 in July 1984, which was later relocated at the Container Terminal in 1989. A new Windward Fruit Terminal with a storage capacity of 60,000 square feet was built at berth 101 in 1992 for Geest Line who, after being taken over by Fyffes Line, moved to Portsmouth in 1995. The site was then redeveloped as a new passenger facility, the City Cruise Terminal in 2001, which was upgraded in 2007.

The Windward Terminal at berth 101 with the vessel *Geest St Lucia* discharging bananas to the temperature controlled store.

Berth 104 saw the building of a new Canary Islands Fruit Terminal. Constructed by a local company Conder Structures, it was officially opened in December 1991 and afforded 108,000 square feet of covered storage. The building has recently been earmarked for redevelopment as the latest Cruise Terminal.

The centre section of the sheds at berths 105/106 were replaced with a new terminal built by the contractor Monk. The reinforced concrete construction began in 1959 and was officially opened the following year by Field Marshall the Rt. Hon. Viscount Slim on 29th November. It became the Mayflower Cruise Terminal, principally for the use of P&O line vessels *Canberra* and *Oriana* in its early days. It has since undergone several transformations and upgrades over the years, the most recent being in 2003.

The contractor's advertisement for the new terminal building at berths 105/106 opened in 1960. (Dave Marden Collection)

Further along the quay, a new Cold Store was built at berth 108 in 1957, replacing its predecessor that stood at berth 40 until being destroyed in the war. Having opened for business on 17th January 1958 with the arrival of the *Brisbane Star* from New Zealand, it operated until falling out of use in 1982, due to most frozen cargoes being transported in refrigerated containers.

A new Cold Store was built at berth 108, replacing the former facility destroyed at berth 40 during the war. (Jeff Pain Collection)

One noteworthy change of dock usage in the New (Western) Docks was the introduction of flying boat services. The British Marine Air Navigation Company was a joint operation between Supermarine and Southern Railways, with flights from Woolston to the Channel Islands and Cherbourg from 1923, the firm becoming Imperial Airways in 1924. The service ran until 1929 when land based aircraft took over the routes.

Imperial Airways began flights from Southampton Docks in 1937 with flying boats using a pontoon at berth 101 in the Western Docks and, in the following year, a new mooring and terminal was built at berth 109, the administration building being Imperial House. The services operated to Alexandria and South Africa, but on the outbreak of war they transferred to Poole.

The Imperial Airways landing stage at berth 101 pictured in May 1938. The ship behind it is the Lamport & Holt vessel *Voltaire.*

Imperial Airways flying boat *Centurian* taxis in front of the North German Lloyd ship *General von Stueben* at berth 101 in 1938. (Jeff Pain Collection)

Imperial Airways aircraft at their 'new' terminal at berth 109 in 1938. (Dave Marden Collection)

The pre-war wooden clad Imperial House at berth 109 which served as the Imperial Airways Terminal building. Note the precarious 'conning tower' in this 1947 photograph.

12. The King George V Graving Dock

The final phase of the New Docks Extension was the construction of the King George V Graving Dock – then the world's largest drydock and capable of accommodating the biggest vessels afloat. With the building of the New Docks well advanced, work commenced in January 1931, the joint contractors being John Mowlem & Co. and Edmund Nuttall. Once again this mammoth undertaking involved the use of railways and locomotives. In this instance there were 19 engines employed by Mowlem.

While the New Docks had been created by reclamation, the drydock project reverted to the earlier method of building a huge embankment across the seaward end of the site and then excavating inside it. In all, two million tons of earth was removed, the spoil being loaded into hopper barges via a temporary jetty and disposed of down in the Solent.

The works lasted three years and, while the official opening was performed by the monarch himself on 26th July 1933, some ancillary and remedial works continued for another year or so. During that time 750,000 tons of concrete were poured into the man-made crater and, on completion, the dock measured 1,200 feet long and 165 feet wide, with an entrance width of 135 feet. The floor is 25 feet thick and the height of the walls from floor to cope level is 59 feet 6 inches. Four 1,250 horsepower, 54 inch diameter pumps were installed to drain the dock. In addition, with a similar arrangement to the station at berth 101, storm water pumping was installed to relieve flooding in the Millbrook area.

The hollow steel caisson, or sliding gate, was 138 feet 6 inches long, 58 feet 6 inches high and 29 feet thick. When partly filled with water as ballast, the caisson weighed 4,600 tons and was hauled into a recess to allow movement of ships in and out of the dock.

At the time of the works, plans were in hand for a possible second drydock alongside this one and, as a consequence, a duplicate electricity control panel was installed in readiness, but the new dock was never constructed and the KGV became the final drydock to be built at Southampton.

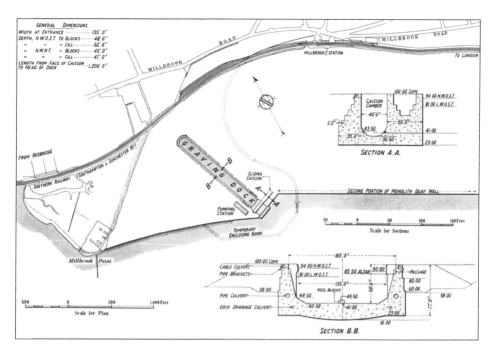

A diagram showing the position of the drydock and the temporary bank that enclosed the works. The main dimensions of both the drydock and the caisson chamber are also given. (Dave Marden Collection)

As a prelude to the works, two gigantic steam navvies gained access to the site via a level crossing at Church Lane, Millbrook on 21st June 1931.

The two steam navvies, having crossed the railway line, make their ponderous way to the drydock site.

The bleak panorama at the Millbrook site as work begins on the enclosing embankment. The small huts of the isolation hospital are in the centre of the photograph taken on 15th May 1931.

One of the first stages of the drydock construction was the completion of the enclosing embankment, seen here on 2nd September 1931.

The contractor's temporary railway runs along the top of the enclosing embankment as dredgers toil in the distance. (Bert Moody Collection)

The sluice gates in the embankment are in place to control the tidal waters on 29th June 1931.

A contractor's train dumping spoil into a barge from a temporary jetty adjoining the surrounding embankment. The hopper barges disposed of the material in deep water in the Solent.

Inside the embankment excavations are under way on the floor of the new drydock as cranes and trains work on the preliminary trenches.

Work in progress on the drydock floor and caisson chamber.

With the caisson chamber walls completed, the interior is removed by crane into rail wagons for disposal.

Lots of activity as the drydock floor is made ready for the concrete on 7th January 1932.

Looking westwards across the caisson chamber on 14th March 1932 with the enclosing embankment as a backdrop to the scene.

The view from the embankment looking north up the drydock towards the drydock head.

An aerial view taken on 28th October 1932 puts the huge expanse of the site into perspective. The spoil jetty and enclosing embankment are to the right, while the works on the New Docks quays are shown at the top of the picture.

The steelwork and early stages of the drydock pumping station which also served as an important electricity substation on the docks internal network.

The trenches and shuttering are in place to form the east and head walls of the dock on 13th November 1932.

The gravel washing plant at the drydock site where continuous wagon loads were cleaned before being used in the tons of concrete mixed on the site.

The contractor's railway runs a train of concrete hopper wagons around the site as the huge walls take shape.

The everlasting trains of concrete hopper wagons dispose of their loads on 24th December 1932.

Looking westwards across completion with the walls and floor of the drydock almost finished in this photograph taken on 7th February 1933.

Break time for some as the dock is completed on 31st May 1933. Workers rest precariously on the dock head steps. The Toogoods depot and Millbrook railway goods shed are in the background.

With the major works completed on 31st May 1933 the drydock is flooded, via a 24 inch diameter pipe, with seawater pumped from the dredger *Foremost Chief*. Towering behind the rubble is the last of the New Docks monoliths, laden with cast-iron blocks as it sinks into position.

Officials look on from the floor of the drydock as the water cascades into the caisson chamber. Presumably the flooding of the drydock was a slow process but the workman at the bottom has already got his feet wet.

With the drydock flooded up to sea level, the dredger *Foremost 49* claws away the enclosing bank to let in the tide on 11th June 1933.

Preparations are under way for the grand opening by His Royal Highness King George V as temporary stands are erected all around the drydock. This is the west side on the 11th July 1933.

A view of the east side stands from where the royal party will be seated for the opening ceremony. There are now just 15 days to go.

It is 26th July 1933 and the big day arrives in summer sunshine as their Majesties King George V and Queen Mary disembark from the Royal Yacht *Victoria & Albert* flanked by Mr Gerald Loader, Chairman of Southern Railway, on the left and Sir Herbert Walker, General Manager of Southern Railway on the right. The Duchess of York is seen behind them.

Following the opening ceremony, the Queen pours a goblet of Empire wine upon the flower decked waters of the dock.

Although the dock was officially declared open on 26th July 1933 it was unusable until the steel entrance caisson was in place. Here we see it being floated into its chamber on the 28th August.

Looking westwards to the drydock pumping station across the newly installed caisson on 11th September 1933.

It is now 2nd November 1933 and works continue around the drydock with the rails for the 50 ton crane being installed on the west side of the dock.

The new 50 ton Stothert & Pitt crane under construction on the west side of the drydock on 11th May 1934.

At last all is ready as the drydock and its workforce await the arrival of the first vessel in for overhaul. This was the White Star Line's *Majestic* on 19th January 1934. At that time, it was the world's largest ship entering the world's largest drydock. The area beyond the drydock, at the rear of the pumping house, has still to be reclaimed.

Anxious faces peer over the sides of the *Majestic* as the liner inches into the drydock. This view was presumably taken from the ship's bridge on 19th January 1934.

Seen from the air, the *Majestic* glides into the King George V Drydock on 19th January 1934. (Bert Moody Collection)

Job done as the towering *Majestic* sits on the blocks on 20th January 1934 and the first drydocking is complete.

The River Test is a hive of activity as the *Queen Mary* makes her first venture into the new drydock on 27th March 1936. The *Majestic* is laid up at berth 108. (Dave Marden Collection)

The massive drydock caisson required periodic maintenance and on such occasions it was taken from its chamber and floated down to one of the other drydocks in the Old (Eastern) Docks where it was cleaned and repaired in the same manner as a ship. A series of photographs was taken to illustrate the process in 1954.

From 1989 the King George V graving dock became the last remaining drydock in use and saw spasmodic occupation until 2008 when the caisson gate was badly in need of repairs. With the costs not being commercially viable the caisson was taken away for scrap and the dock remains permanently flooded as a wet dock.

The caisson is carefully floated out of its chamber on 5th March 1954.

After being hauled clear of its chamber the caisson is positioned upright inside the flooded drydock.

Left: Two days later, on 7th March 1954, the caisson is then turned over on its side.

Below: The Docks Engineers Department workforce poses for the occasion on 7th March 1954.

A murky morning on 9th March 1954 as the caisson is towed through the drydock entrance on the start of its journey.

Tugs manoeuvre the caisson ready to tow it down the River Test and around Dock Head to the Outer Dock. The jetty in the distance is at Millbrook Point.

The Caisson being towed into the Outer Dock on 9th March 1954.

The blocks in No.3 Drydock are in position to form a cradle on which the caisson will sit.

The drydock is now flooded and the tugs position the caisson for entry on 9th March 1954.

On 10th March 1954 the dock is pumped dry and the caisson sits on the blocks ready for its 'spring clean'.

Part Four – The Docks in Wartime

13. The Second World War

For much of its earlier years Southampton Docks was a major embarkation point for troops sailing to overseas campaigns. As mentioned in the Railway Chapter, such movements were colossal and regular, particularly during the First World War. However, the Second World War brought the conflict to our own shores and, like many other British towns and cities, Southampton suffered considerable bomb damage from the early 1940s. The docks and its attendant industries was a prime target, where some of the early buildings, by then around a century old, were destroyed, as were many of the recent constructions at the New (Western) Docks completed less than a decade beforehand.

From the outbreak of war in 1939 most passenger services were diverted to less vulnerable ports and Southampton relied mainly on coastal traffic. A build-up of troops and equipment as a bridgehead for the British Expeditionary Force took place, but this was stepped down following the fall of France. The huge floating drydock at berth 50 was transported to Portsmouth Harbour in 1940 but Southampton's other drydocks were kept busy with repairs to vessels damaged by mines, etc.

The most serious aerial attacks occurred in the summer of 1940 and through the following winter but, although there was much devastation to buildings, much of the port's quays and drydocks remained intact or suffered superficial damage. In total there were 69 air raids which destroyed 23 transit sheds and warehouses while many others were repaired and brought back into use, and throughout the war years some 4,300,000 troops with 3,900,000 tons of equipment passed over the quaysides.

Despite the air raids, the docks was able to maintain its operations, although in a much different role. From 1942 it became the arrival point for much needed food, supplies and equipment from America. The docks themselves were taken over by the military who utilised the sheds, stores and offices for a variety of purposes as well as setting up barrage balloon stations, boom defences and gun emplacements. During the build up to D-Day in 1944 the docks facilities were chiefly engaged in the construction of floating Mulberry Harbours and the assembly of huge convoys of landing crafts ready for the invasion of France.

The latter end of the war saw several hundreds of German prisoners of war landed at Southampton and marched off to various camps in the area. One of these was adjacent to the New Docks main gate No.8 and many of the occupants seemed very pleased to be there, away from the perils of wartime.

With the war over, a sense of normality came about in 1945 with the return of several ocean liners, most notably the *Queen Mary* on 11th August, while on the 20th of that month, the *Queen Elizabeth* arrived in port for the first time, after serving as a troopship since 1941, making her maiden commercial voyage on 16th October 1946.

One of the most notable victims of bombing was the International Cold Store at berth 40. From 13th August 1940 fire crews were in attendance for several weeks as vast quantities of molten butter continued to burn. (Bert Moody Collection)

The stark remains of M warehouse at berth 12 in the Inner Docks following successive air raids on 30th November and 2nd December 1940. (Bert Moody Collection)

Another victim of enemy bombs was D warehouse at berth 10 in the Inner Docks, taking a direct hit on 26th September 1940. The building in the centre background is the former National Provincial Bank, now converted to apartments. (Bert Moody Collection)

A different view of the remains of D warehouse on 26th September 1940, taken from M warehouse, itself a victim just two months later. The Continental Booking Office at berth 9 can be seen top left. (Bert Moody Collection)

Little was left of the Canadian Pacific's offices after bombing on 23rd November 1940. The building stood adjacent to the Canute Road railway crossing into the Old (Eastern) Docks and was replaced in the 1962 by a modern Dock House which was the administration centre of the dock owners, by then the British Transport Docks Board. (Bert Moody Collection)

Enemy bombing was not confined to the docks. The Royal Pier was severely damaged. Note the landing craft at the centre right of the picture.

Looking north from the Royal Pier where the elbow at the end of the covered walkway has been blasted away.

The bomb damage seen from the north shows the Tea Rooms (left) and the Pavilion almost cut off from the shore.

Another angle shows the missing section of the Royal Pier.

The quayside at 101 berth suffered damage by bombing and a huge crack can be seen there on 12th May 1942. (Bert Moody Collection)

Inside 101 shed where wartime bombs had destroyed the nearly new building, pictured on 12th May 1942. (Bert Moody Collection)

The rear of berth 101 at the New Docks showing damage to both the transit shed and the railway tracks on 12th May 1942. (Bert Moody Collection)

Many dock premises were victims of bombing raids. The motor components factory of A.C. Delco was severely damaged but much of the steelwork was recovered for recycling in the war effort. This photograph was taken on 24th March 1942.

Another scene from A.C. Delco on 24th March 1942, where bricks are being cleaned and recycled for later use in rebuilding.

Southampton's ship repair facilities were kept at full stretch during the war. This is SS *Hartlepool*, seen in No 7 drydock on 21st October 1940 after suffering a torpedo attack which blew off its stern off Portland on 5th July that year. (Bert Moody Collection)

More shipping damage, this time to the *SS Harpagus*, being inspected by the docks workforce and pictured in the New Docks for repair on 13th September 1944. (Bert Moody Collection)

A fleet of landing craft along the quays at the New (Western) Docks on 22nd December 1943. The cranes have been moved away to provide easy access. (Bert Moody Collection)

More landing craft, this time assembled in the Empress Dock prior to D-Day in 1944. (Bert Moody Collection)

Following the D-Day landings in 1944, stores were shipped across the Channel to Normandy. This activity is seen here at the Western Docks. (Bert Moody Collection)

A section of the Mulberry Harbour under construction in the Old (Eastern) Docks, photographed on 8th November 1944. (Bert Moody Collection)

More of the Mulberry Harbour, here seen being floated out of No.7 (King George V) Drydock with attendant wartime vessels on 18th May 1944. (Bert Moody Collection)

The scene at the Town Quay where wartime vessels congregated on 5th October 1944. (Bert Moody Collection)

During the latter part of the Second World War supplies and equipment were ferried across to France from a terminal built on the western side of the King George V Drydock. Here, an ambulance train is being taken aboard the Southern Railway's *Hampton Ferry.*

The D-Day landing craft turned to other duties after the 1944 invasion. They are seen in this photograph landing German prisoners who were being escorted ashore at the Royal Pier in March 1945. (Bert Moody Collection)

Another landing point for German PoWs was adjacent to the 101 berth pumping station (now the western end of Mayflower Park). The US forces keep a close watch as they troop ashore on 13th March 1945. (Bert Moody Collection)

The sign points the way for the PoW Cage near the main New Docks gate No.8 on 11th September 1944. (Bert Moody Collection)

Smiling faces from some of the captives as they march off to confinement at the 8 Gate camp on 11th September 1944. (Bert Moody Collection)

The scene inside the cage near 101 berth on 13th October 1944 where German Prisoners of War were held and processed for confinement. (Bert Moody Collection)

Peacetime returns and this view from April 1946 shows a passenger boat train departing from berth 44 with the *Queen Mary* still in her wartime grey.

One of the most fascinating stories of Southampton Docks in wartime concerns the damage to N warehouse, following its ruin during an air raid on 30th November 1940. Unlike many such buildings that were merely bulldozed away, the vault below ground level was redeveloped as a heavily fortified control centre in 1942. The bomb-proof bunker was 100 feet long by 84 feet wide and contained telecommunications equipment, along with offices, rest rooms and workshops. The building had an auxiliary power plant which supplied heating and ventilation.

After the end of the war it was judged too solid to demolish and was largely used as a store, then latterly as a charity shop, while a more modern docks telephone exchange was built above it in the 1960s. After having been abandoned in the 1990s, modern concrete-busting equipment finally put paid to it and the site was redeveloped for apartments in 2003.

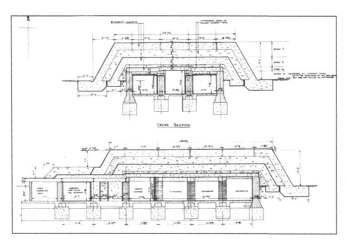

A profile of the N Vault Control Centre construction showing the various layers of protective concrete and sand. (Dave Marden Collection)

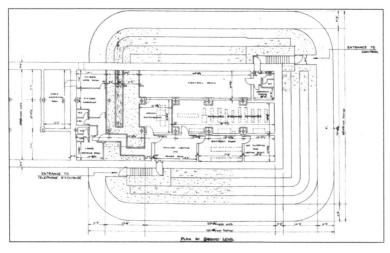

A plan of the N Vault structure detailing the various rooms and facilities below the concrete casing. (Dave Marden Collection)

The remains of the ill-fated N Warehouse after being bombed on 30th November 1940, where the site was rebuilt as a control centre for both the docks and the military operations in the region. (Bert Moody Collection)

Work on the control centre began with strengthening the remaining vault of the former N warehouse before the outer bomb-proof structure could be built above it.

Some of the massive steel reinforcement laid down before the pouring of concrete.

The first roof layer covering the old vault is ready for concrete. The remains of M warehouse stand in the background.

Phase one of the control centre shows the first level of concrete is in place over the former brick vault, but a much sturdier outer skin of sand and more reinforced concrete would be built over this.

One of the two blast-proof entrances showing the thickness of the reinforced concrete where heavy steel doors would be fitted.

The shuttering and steelwork is in place on the north side of the building ready for another extremely hefty bastion of concrete.

A thick layer of sand was placed between the inner and outer layers of concrete to cushion any blast.

Another shell of brickwork was applied to contain the sand between the two concrete layers.

The brickwork skin is now in place and ready for the outer concrete shell to be applied over it.

The upper section of the building begins to take shape as the steelwork is readied for yet more concrete.

The final outer casing of concrete is applied to the north side of the building.

One of the ventilation shafts takes shape. Air would be pumped around the building by motors below.

The mixing of concrete was an immense task for the contract workers on their site to the south of the former National Provincial Bank.

Another thick layer of sand is applied to the roof before the final concrete capping is built over it.

The south-east corner of the building takes shape with one of the brick ventilation shafts completed.

More exterior works in progress. The pipes on the right corner of the building are exhausts from the machinery and generators below.

The huge structure taking shape in the final stages of the upper capping.

A later view of this impregnable structure showing its location among the ruins about it. In the middle distance is the Harland & Wolff works at the Trafalgar Drydock.

The job is almost complete as the mammoth concrete edifice stands like a pharaoh's tomb.

A final view of the finished building with the debris around it now largely cleared. The shell of M warehouse, with its exposed floor supports, stands forlorn by the Inner Dock, while the chimneys in the right foreground represent the remains of the former Canadian Pacific Company offices on Canute Road.

Left: The heartbeat of the control centre with its generators.

Below: The underground nerve centre with its personnel safe from enemy attack.

The other end of the Control Room offers a few home comforts during brief periods of rest from enemy actions and the running of the docks.

A glimpse of the (then) modern telephone and communications equipment.

Left: The telephone exchange switchboard at the Control Centre was of the extending jack plug variety. Right: Girls manning the telephone switchboard and providing vital links with the outside world.

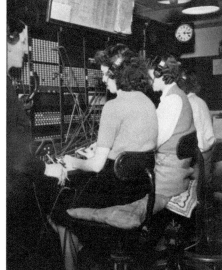

Part Five – The Container Port

14. The First Container Berths

The opening of the King George V Drydock and the completion of the New (Western) Docks extension had marked the end of an era. With the advent of war, and in the years of austerity that followed, there was neither the incentive nor the finance to go further. Public ownership of the docks from 1st January 1948 was mainly concerned with repairs, maintenance and replacement of facilities lost in the conflict. There was only one prestigious project, that of building a new Ocean Terminal at berths 43/4, which was opened in 1950, and no new major works of expansion to the quays were carried out until the first container berths were constructed.

In the 1960s the mode of shipping and cargo handling was changing to containerisation. In consequence plans were announced in 1965 for a £60 million extension to the New Docks which were renamed the Western Docks at that time. Under the new scheme, additional quays would stretch up the River Test from the King George V Drydock to Redbridge. A parliamentary Bill was passed on 9th August 1966 and authorisation was given to the new works on 25th January 1967.

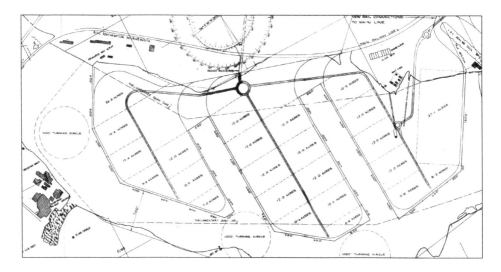

As with earlier extensions of the docks, there were many schemes submitted before the final plan was chosen. One grand design proposed 20,850 feet of new quays backed by over 300 acres of storage area. Stretching almost across to the Marchwood shoreline where the main channel provided for three 1,000 foot turning circles for vessels, which, by today's standards, would have now been totally inadequate.

The area to be developed was mainly salt marshes where creeks such as Tanners Brook found their way from the city to the River Test. As in the days of the Western Docks construction, the creeks were culverted and disappeared beneath a layer of concrete, though for many years the unmade area at the rear of the berths remained in a natural state until comparatively recent times when it was surfaced and extended as a storage area for vehicles and containers.

Above: The Millbrook mudlands before the building of the Container Port. The Southampton to Bournemouth railway snakes along the left of the picture, passing the former Redbridge Sleeper Depot before it crosses the River Test. To the north is the P&O ship *Canberra* in the King George V Drydock. Top centre is Marchwood Power Station and Eling quay is at the bottom right.

Opposite page: This plan for the proposed container port drawn up in 1965 included railway connections to the quays. Only phase one of the scheme (later berths 201/2) was adopted and the remainder redesigned. (Dave Marden Collection)

The construction method for the container berths was much simpler than all that had been employed previously, consisting of a line of interlocking steel piles topped with a concrete coping and backed by a surface of pre-cast Stelcon concrete slabs, each 6 feet 8 inches square and 5.5 inches thick, bedded on gravel. There was a minor variation at berth 207 where contractor Nuttalls used a combination of steel tubes with interlocking piles between them.

The first stage of the container berth would bring a new quay, of 900 feet in length, backed with 20 acres of land for container handling with specialised equipment. Dredging commenced in February 1967 and the berth, originally numbered 111/112, was completed the following year when the Belgian Line vessel *Teniers* became the first to use the new facility on 27th October 1968.

New cranes stand at the ready on berth 111 while construction work on the first container berth continues behind them in 1968. On the right of the photograph is the pumping station of the King George V Drydock.

On 4th December 1969 the *Atlantic Causeway* sailed from the container port on her maiden voyage and soon afterwards, the quay was extended by a further 900 feet to provide a second berth. To emphasise their significance, berth numbers 111/112 were changed to 201, and the extension became berth 202 to differentiate them from the rest of the docks. The first vessel to call at the new berth was the *Kamakura Maru* on 29th January 1972.

Berths 111/112. The very first container quay at Southampton in operation in December 1969, has Atlantic Container Line's *Atlantic Causeway* awaiting her maiden voyage. Work is still in progress on laying down the surfacing of the marshalling area and the berth would soon be doubled in length.

The massive container port begins to grow. 111/112 Berths (later renumbered 201) are already in use as berths 202, 203, 204 and 205 on the right of the photograph are taking shape. (Jim Brown Collection)

Berths 111/112 (201) are in operation while berth 202 is almost complete as the cranes there take shape. (Jim Brown Collection)

15. Expansion of the Container Port

Overseas Containers, subsequently P&O Containers, together with Ben Line and Associated Containers, announced their intention to use Southampton as the sole UK port for their Far East services due to commence in 1972, and approval was obtained for the provision of an additional 3,900 feet of quays (berths 203-206). Work commenced with contractors Laing in June 1970 and the original prospective operators were joined by Trio Lines, an amalgamation of Hapag Lloyd, Nippon Yusen Kaisha and Mitsui OSK Lines. The newly completed berth 204 was first used on 29th January 1972 by Overseas Container Line's *Tokyo Bay* and, of the additional berths, 206 was first occupied in May 1978 by vessels of the South Africa Conference Lines.

Contractors Laing pile driving at berth 204 on 1st February 1971.

An early stage of the works at berth 204 in August 1971 with steel piling for the quay walls in place. On the right of the picture is the former Marchwood Power Station which was demolished in the early 1990s. (Jim Brown)

The former jetty of Millbrook Sailing Club is seen in this photograph. During the construction of berth 204 it was covered by the new works and still lies beneath the surface of the Container Port. (Jim Brown Collection)

Another photograph from August 1971 shows the Canteen and Administration Blocks taking shape at berth 204. (Jim Brown Collection)

Works advancing at berth 204 on 4th October 1971 with the dredger *WD Challenger* in the background.

The container berth on 3rd August 1971 is a sea of aggregate with the first two cranes for berth 204 under construction. (Jim Brown Collection)

Reclamation for the container berths continues on 5th August 1971 as the area for berths 204 and 205 takes shape. (Jim Brown)

Surfacing works at berth 204 berth in August 1971 with the laying of prefabricated Stelcon concrete slabs. (Jim Brown)

Below: An aerial view showing the growing Container Port with cranes on the completed berths 201 and 202. Berth 204 is also operational while berth 205 is under construction and 206 is already taking shape.

The berths at 204 and 205 were completed in 1972 and are seen occupied during their early days. Berth 201 and 202 are at the top of the photograph but the angled berth at 203 is yet to be occupied by cable ships for some years. (Jim Brown Collection)

The construction works at 206 berth ahead of its opening in May 1978.

The new Container Clearance Depot at the rear of berth 206 on 2nd June 1978.

Even the huge SA *Waterberg* at berth 206 in the early 1980s is overshadowed by the towering portainer cranes, while straddle carriers wait to take away the landed containers. (Dave Marden)

The container stacking area at the rear of berth 206 was extended by 15 acres during 1992-93 which increased storage capacity by 25 per cent. The work was carried out by contractor John Mowlem. (Jim Brown)

New cranes being built at berth 207 in summer 1993. Three were constructed over a period of 14 weeks at a cost of £9 million. When complete, the cranes were moved from the site to the quayside on specialised bogies. (Jim Brown Collection)

One of the new cranes being manoeuvred into position on the quayside. (Jim Brown Collection)

Solent Container Services held an open day on 2nd June 1996 when the public were allowed onto the container port to see how things were done. This photograph shows demonstrations of lifting by straddle carriers. (Jim Brown Collection)

By December 1996 the quays were being extended still further to provide berth No.207, adding another 1,378 feet and increasing the total provision to 4,429 feet, with the first ship to use the new berth being the *Shenzhen Bay* which called on 23rd December 1996. The Container Port was now operated by Southampton Container Terminals, jointly owned by P&O Containers and Associated British Ports who had assumed ownership of the rest of the Port in 1982.

A photograph from May 1996 shows piling at berth 207. The work was carried out by contractor Edmund Nuttall and provided an additional 1,378 feet of quayside. (Jim Brown Collection)

The view across berth 206 stacking area looking across to the 20 gate road bridge at left centre of the photograph. The Maritime Freightliner Depot stretches across the centre of the picture. (Jim Brown)

Berth 207 nearing completion in November 1996. (Jim Brown Collection)

A number of streams ran into the River Test before the construction of the Container Port. One of these, Tanner's Brook, is seen being culverted in 1997 when the area was filled and surfaced for container storage. (Jim Brown Collection)

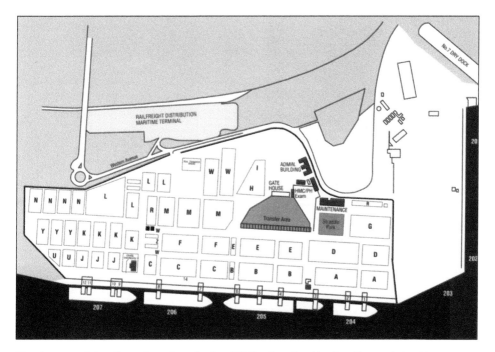

The layout of the Container Port in the 1990s showing the berths and stacking areas. (Jim Brown Collection)

The container port looking eastwards with the unmade '208 berth' in the foreground, this being just a bank along the shallow water with no quays to accommodate vessels. The area behind it is used for the storage of containers and imported vehicles.

With more space required for cargo handling the remaining area between 207 berth and Redbridge was developed and surfaced for the storage of containers and imported vehicles but the quayside, unofficially referred to as 208 berth, has only an embankment at the waters edge. No quay wall has been constructed there and the tidal water remains undredged. This extension also absorbed the old Redbridge Railway Works which were purchased by ABP in March 1994. The soil in this area had been heavily saturated with creosote and chemicals during its railway days but a lengthy process of decontamination was carried out before its use for vehicle storage. A small area at the western end of the site was converted to a riverside park and given over to the City Council in September 2002.

In the midst of the new developments was 203 berth, an angled quay between berths 202 and 204 on the corner of the Container Port. This had been occupied in November 1974 by the Post Office Central Marine Depot which dealt with the laying of submarine cables and occupied a five acre site between the two container activities. The operation was taken over by BT Marine on 1st October 1987, and afterwards by Cable & Wireless 1994 who later transferred to Portland. In November 2006 the berth was equipped with a new 100 tonne crane for handling containers from smaller feeder ships.

The cable laying ship *C S Iris* alongside the BT Marine Depot at berth 203 in the 1980s. The vessel's bow is adapted for the distribution of cable on to the seabed. On the left is the gantry for loading the miles of cable on to the ship. (Dave Marden)

For the first time in the history of Southampton Docks, no railway connection was made to the new quays. In fact, the whole of the container docks were devoid of railways. However, a large railway marshalling yard, the Maritime Freightliner Depot, was built at the rear of berths 205/6 where specialised equipment took the containers from the quays to flat wagons for distribution around the country.

The Freightliner Depot and marshalling yards as seen from the air in 2004. The bridge at the top of the picture is the road to Millbrook and Dock gate 20.

Looking eastwards at the Freightliner Distribution Depot at Millbrook where containers are assembled for railway transportation. The Southampton to Bournemouth main line is on the left. (Dave Marden)

As an illustration of the increasing draft of vessels in recent years, the depth of water at low tide at the container port is 40 feet at 201/2, 42 feet at 204-6 and 49 feet 2in at 207. Due to the increased size of container ships, berths 201/2 could no longer handle the larger vessels and for several years were given over to the vehicle trade with the area behind used for storing them. But authorisation was given in 2011 for the two original berths to be rebuilt with a depth of 52.5 feet of water at low tide so that they will be able to accommodate the latest generation of container ships as part of an £80 million upgrade. Work is expected to be completed by the end of 2013.

The busy Container Port in 2004. At that time, berths 201/2 in the foreground were used for vehicle storage, but will now revert to container operations.

Part Six - The Railway Years

16. The Importance of the Railways

Railways played a leading part in the development and growth of Southampton Docks. Firstly, there were the locomotives of the various contractors involved in the various stages of construction. These played a key role in the movement of spoil and materials during in the building of much of what we still see today. But, more importantly, there were the locomotives and stock of the companies that owned the docks, from the Southampton Dock Company, the L&SWR and Southern Railway, through to the nationalised days of British Railways. Those were times when most heavy goods were moved around the country by railway, either to individual firms who each had their own sidings, or to freight yards where trains were marshalled for local and area distribution.

Mention has already been made in the earlier chapters regarding the many contractor's locomotives used in building the docks but it was some time before the Southampton Dock Company brought in engines themselves. From the early days, horses had hauled wagons around the docks and trains were assembled before being taken across Canute Road to the Town Yard, where the L&SWR would take them off to the capital or elsewhere on its network. It wasn't until 1865 that the Dock Company invested in the first locomotive of its own and an odd collection of engines had been acquired by the time the L&SWR purchased the docks in 1892.

A typical four-wheeled contractor's locomotive at work during the early excavations for the White Star Dock in 1908. (Jeff Pain Collection)

173

Another contractor's locomotive busy at the White Star Dock in 1910. On the left are the workshops of ship repairers Harland & Wolff while the South Western Hotel dominates the skyline on the right. (Bert Moody Collection)

One of the Southampton Dock Company's early locomotives was *Canute*, purchased new in 1870 from the firm of Dick & Stevenson of Airdrie and pictured in the docks on 28th June 1901. (Dave Marden Collection)

The Southampton Dock Company's final locomotive purchases were made in 1890. This was *Clausentum* built that year by R&W Hawthorn, Leslie & Co. (Bert Moody Collection)

Ironside was a sister engine to *Clausentum* and survived beyond its Dock Company ownership by lasting well into the days of British Railways. It is seen here at Guildford Shed in the late 1940s. (Dave Marden Collection)

The Dock Company engines were replaced by a fleet of fourteen B4 class shunters from 1893, being purpose built by the LSWR. For the most part, these handled the docks internal movements until after the Second World War, when an equal number of the distinctive former US Army Transportation Corps tank engines were purchased by the Southern Railway in 1947, being surplus after the conflict. The USA locos gave sterling work until they themselves were eventually superseded by a further batch of 14 diesels from 1962 and these saw out the final years of shunters based in the docks. Throughout this period, the docks engines were housed in a running shed adjacent to No.3 Drydock, although a handful were later stationed in the New (Western) Docks until around 1979.

The LSWR introduced the B4 class shunting locomotives to the docks in 1893. The engines originally carried names of ports served by the railway company ships. *Havre*, built in 1891 arrived in 1896 and is pictured behind Central Road where one the shops at the rear was still showing war damage on 2nd August 1947. (Dave Marden Collection)

One of Southampton Docks B4 class locomotives No.96 *Normandy* seen shunting in the Eastern Docks in Southern Railway days. (Dave Marden Collection)

A fleet of 14 former USA Transportation Corps tank locos were drafted into the docks after the Second World War. Southern Railway No.73 was built in 1943 and came to the docks in 1947 where it was photographed on 2nd August that year. (Dave Marden Collection)

One of the USA tanks in later years. No.30069 was photographed near No.4 Drydock on 7th September 1961. (J.H. Aston)

Built in 1962 by the Lincoln firm of Ruston & Hornsby, this diesel locomotive No. D2994 was one of 14 supplied to the docks in 1962 where it posed for the camera on 20th April 1963. (Dave Marden Collection)

Ruston Diesel loco No.07010 picks its way through the parked cars near No.5 Gate in the Eastern Docks on 18th July 1975. (Dave Marden)

A cavalcade of docks shunters parades alongside the *SS Canberra* at No.7 Drydock in July 1962. None of the old Dock Company locos had survived but E2 class engines (second right) regularly worked in the Western Docks in the 1950s. (Bert Moody Collection)

The sheer scale of goods and passengers transported through the docks cannot be overstated, during both peacetime and in periods of conflict. Many people will still recall the seemingly endless trains of banana wagons being hauled off to the markets of London and beyond, while the prodigious boat trains transported the rich and famous (and those not so wealthy) to and from the various terminals around the docks.

In 1871 a total of 2,362 ships called at the docks, where over 500 wagons per week (annual total 26,882) were used in transporting goods. A further 3,483 wagons of coal also arrived that year to fuel vessels, mostly steamships at that time, along with another 10,000 trucks of mail. These totals had practically doubled just two years later.

From 1894 the docks provided facilities for troopships, where, apart from during the various wars, troop traffic flowed from September until April in maintaining the Empire. Troop trains also added considerably to rail traffic at these times, which lasted until the end of 1962. During the South African War of 1899 to 1902 some 528,000 troops and 27,922 horses with appropriate stores passed through the port.

During the First World War the figures were over seven million troops, 850,000 horses and 180,000 vehicles, and additionally, many ambulance trains were operated. To accommodate the sheer scale of these movements Canute Road was closed to vehicular traffic and a footbridge was erected over the railway crossing for pedestrians.

An early 1900s freight train enters the Old (Eastern) Docks headed by LSWR 4-4-0 L11 class locomotive No.441. (Historical Model Railway Society Collection)

Railway excursions to the docks were popular during the late 1920s and early 1930s when visitors came by train from all parts of the country to view the mighty passenger liners, and also to marvel at the massive dock extension works taking place at the West Bay.

Over the various eras of its growth, vast marshalling yards were built in both the Old (Eastern) and New (Western) Docks to handle the enormous amounts of railway traffic. In the Eastern Docks were the Empress and Test Yards, while the Western Docks boasted three huge shunting grounds at the rear of berths 103, 104 and 107, and at its peak the total mileage of tracks on the docks estate was almost 78 miles – enough to stretch from Southampton to London! The dock lines served every berth and quayside shed, allowing smooth transit of passengers and freight from ship to destination.

When the clouds of war returned in 1939 regular passenger services ceased but the embarkation of the British Expeditionary Force saw around 800,000 troops and 300,000 tons of stores handled during the early months of the war, throughout which the docks were largely handed over to the military. During the massive build-up to the D-Day operations nearly four million troops and prisoners of war were transported, mainly by rail, through the docks.

In peacetime some of the figures for railway traffic are also quite astonishing. Over the Friday and Saturday of the August bank holiday weekend of 1932 some 78 boat trains were handled in those 48 hours. On a single day in June 1933 a total of 976 goods wagons left the docks during a 19 hour period – 424 of these being loaded with bananas. In 1936 the dock railways operated 4,800 passenger trains with another 4,245 carrying freight.

The totals for the 1950s and 1960s are equally impressive: 1955 saw 2,374 boat trains and 5,893 freight trains with the respective figures for 1960 being 2,271 and 5,532. By the mid 1960s the totals began to fall but were still quite remarkable in 1965 with 1,164 and 4,623. By 1973 air travel, containerisation and road haulage had claimed a large share of both passengers and goods traffic, and the number of boat trains had fallen to just 459.

A typical banana train made up of 30 wagons is seen leaving the Eastern Docks bound for London on 2nd May 1958. The train is approaching the Canute Road crossing and the building to the right of the engine is the former Shipping Traffic Office which still stands today.

Boat trains were a common sight in the 1950s and 1960s when this one, The *Cunarder* was pictured leaving the Ocean Terminal for Waterloo with passengers from the *Queen Elizabeth* on 12th May 1964.

Former docks engines occasionally returned there for steam specials. USA Army tanks Nos 30064 and 30073 are seen at the Ocean Terminal with an enthusiasts train bound for Fawley on 19th March 1966. (Bert Moody Collection)

The advent of affordable air travel effectively ended the days of the ocean liners while the juggernaut lorry marked the demise of rail freight. For the first time in the docks history no railway provision was made to the quaysides when the Southampton container berths were built in the late 1960s due to the motorway network that was growing across the nation. Although it is true to say that the number of containers transported by rail is still considerable, and will grow further since the upgrading of the main lines to carry the larger boxes.

With the current popularity of cruising, boat trains are now being revived, although on a much smaller scale from times gone by. Over the passage of time much of the docks railway network has been either removed or built over, and very little remains apart from one branch line serving the Eastern Docks across Canute Road and another entering the Western Docks at Millbrook. The new Ocean Terminal at berths 46 and 47 has no rail connection.

Part Seven – Today and Beyond

17. Changing Times

Since their initial construction, the various docks and quays have undergone many changes, particularly in the Eastern Docks which have altered almost beyond recognition in order to adapt to the modern requirements of trade and cargo handling.

An interesting aerial photograph of the Old (Eastern) Docks taken on 14th June 1949 shows the skeletal remains of the war damaged Cold Store at berth 40 while the Ocean Terminal is under construction at the top left. Ships in the picture are the *Queen Mary* at berth 46/7 and the troopships *Empire Windrush* at berth 44 and *Eastern Prince* at berth 40. On the Test Quays at berth 38/9 is the *Capetown Castle* while on the along the Itchen Quays are the *Arundel Castle*, *Dunera* and *Andes*. Another troopship, the *Empire Orwell* sits in the Empress Dock along with the *El Nil* and the railway vessels *Ringwood* and *Haslemere*. In No.5 drydock is the *Hampton* Ferry and just visible in the Outer Dock are the *Falaise* and *Isle of Guernsey*.

A magnificent summer scene in days gone by with an impressive line-up of ships on view at the Eastern and Western Docks on 25th July 1956. Bottom left is the *Nevasa* at berth 35/6, and moving along the Itchen, at berth 34 is the *San Miguel* with the *Mahronda* behind in No.5 drydock. The *Homeric* is at berth 33 with the Dunera at berth 31. In the Empress Dock is the *Corrales* at berth 24/5 and the *Wave Conquest* at berth 26/7. On the Test Quays, at berth 40 is the *Stratheden*, while the *Queen Elizabeth* lies alongside the Ocean Terminal at berth 43/4. Over at berth 45 is the *Karadeniz* while at berth 46 is the *Iberia* with the *Neptunia* at berth 47. The *Dilwara* is in No.6 Drydock. In the distance, the Western Dock played host to the *Carnarvon* Castle at berth 102, the *Queen Mary* at berth 103/4, the *Athlone Castle* at berth 104 and the *United States* at berth 106. The dock estate is covered with sheds and workshops at every quay along with a mass of railway sidings connecting them all.

The 12th October 1938 marked the 100 years anniversary of the laying of the docks foundation stone and, to commemorate the event, a Centenary Column was unveiled in the New Docks, just inside No.8 Gate. The column featured a globe encircled with signs of the zodiac and topped with a seahorse. The ceremony was conducted by Mr R. Holland-Martin, chairman of the Southern Railway.

Previous photo: The Eastern Docks in May 1996 presents a marked contrast to the previous photograph. The clutter of sheds and buildings have, in the main, given way to open space for the storage of vehicles. Gone also is the Prince of Wales Drydock. The Queen Elizabeth II Terminal remains, as does the shed at berth 41 while grain silos occupy berth 36. Vessels present are Wallenius Lines' *Faust* at berth 34/5 with *Madame Butterfly* at berth 38/9. The Hual ship *Sanwa* is at berth 40 and NYK's *Jingu Maru* is at berth 43.

Above: The unveiling of the Centenary Column before an invited audience at the New Docks on 12th October 1938, conducted by Southern Railway chairman Mr R. Holland-Martin. (Bert Moody Collection)

The Centenary Column stands proudly at the entrance to the New Docks shortly after its unveiling. The globe has now been relocated adjacent to the offices of Associated British Ports at Ocean Gate, while the original Foundation Stone, and the 60th Anniversary Stone, are situated just inside Dock Gate 4. (Bert Moody Collection)

As in the Eastern Docks, huge changes have taken place in the Western Docks where many of the old sheds, buildings and factories have now disappeared, to be replaced with new facilities to meet present day needs. This photograph taken on 13th August 2005 shows a modern industrial estate with quays now adapted for the current boom in the cruise trade.

Another view, this time from 17th May 2004, with the *Aurora* at berth 106. Bulk cargoes have taken over at berths 107/8 and the massive Standard Telephones Cable works has gone. Further on, the King George V Drydock would soon become permanently flooded as a wet berth.

Many may feel that Southampton Docks has now expanded to its full potential but the current boom in cruise liners and ever increasing container trade creates even greater demand on existing space. New and more efficient ways of operation continue to make the best use of what is available but we have seen how, with each new generation, the docks has grown. So what of the future?

The new Ocean Terminal, pictured on 9th May 2009, symbolises the modern port and its up to date facilities, but will there be enough capacity to sustain the continuing growth of the docks?

Since the reclamation of the West Bay and the construction of the New (Western) Docks, the dredged spoil from the main shipping channel and swinging grounds has been continuously pumped ashore at Dibden Bay by the same method, to regain the area as land. This was always assumed to be for further port use but a public enquiry in 2005 rejected its development as a new container port and the future of the entire site is in question. However, the political climate has changed in recent times and the matter may well be revisited again.

Opposite page: A 1963 advertisement for the James Dredging Company showing the floating pipeline running to the shore at Dibden Bay. (Dave Marden Collection)

One argument says the docks estate is quite adequate for current needs, but who knows what the future holds? Certainly, those early entrepreneurs of the mid 1800s could never have imagined such successive expansions would ever be necessary, but they were and may well be so again. As commented in the introduction, it is difficult to imagine what Southampton would have been like without such developments and the town would have been a much different place.

For better or worse, Southampton has relied upon its docks for generations of benefits to the local economy. Without them, would the lower town today be much different to the shores across Southampton Water? – and would those shores welcome the transformation to what they view across to the modern city? Time will tell if the progress of the past is maintained, or whether a lost opportunity is later regretted.

Planning for the future – or just a pipe dream? Dredged material comes ashore at Dibden Bay in 1957. (Dave Marden Collection)

The reclamation of Dibden Bay seen from the air in the 1960s. Hythe Pier is at the bottom right with the chimneys of Marchwood Power Station in the distance.

The proposed Container Port at Dibden Bay would have provided six new berths to the south of Marchwood Military Port, shown at the top of the illustration. The plan was rejected – but will it be revived? (Jim Brown Collection)

ND - #0291 - 270225 - C0 - 234/156/12 - PB - 9781780910628 - Gloss Lamination